ARROW CORPS 5
A HIGHER ADVENTURE

ORDER OF THE ARROW
BOY SCOUTS OF AMERICA

Acclaim Press™
MORLEY, MISSOURI

Acclaim Press
—— *Your Next Great Book* ——

P.O. Box 238
Morley, MO 63767
(573) 472-9800
www.acclaimpress.com

Library of Congress Control Number: 2009932762

ISBN-13: 978-1-935001-23-2
ISBN-10: 1-935001-23-X

First Printing: 2009
Printed in the United States of America
10 9 8 7 6 5 4 3 2 1

ArrowCorps[5]
Commemorative Photo Book

Bradley E. Haddock
Chairman, National Order of the Arrow Committee

Thomas E. Fielder
Adviser, *ArrowCorps*[5] Digital Media Team
National Order of the Arrow Committee

ORDER OF THE ARROW   BOY SCOUTS OF AMERICA

Table of Contents

Dedication

This book is dedicated to those thousands of youth and adult Arrowmen who unselfishly gave up part of their summer to contribute labor in the forest. These distinguished Arrowmen led the Boy Scouts of America to the height of our mission of leadership through unselfish service to others while preserving the beauty of our National Forests for generations to come. We are very proud of and grateful to each individual Arrowman who participated in *ArrowCorps*[5].

Acknowledgements

Every service project in our Brotherhood is, above all, based on the spirit of the Order of the Arrow and our collective history of service. This book is no exception. Led by Robert Mason, Youth Photographer, and Terrel Miller, Videographer, hundreds of Arrowmen contributed more than 80,000 digital images and 110 hours of video from each of the five *ArrowCorps*[5] sites. The contributions of those Arrowmen make *ArrowCorps*[5] the most documented service project in the history of Scouting. Bradley E. Haddock, Chairman of the National Order of the Arrow Committee, personally took the lead in inspiring key members of the National Committee and others in the compilation of this book. We are grateful to all those who contributed to this book including: Michael Hoffman, Vice Chairman, National Events; Clyde Mayer, Order of the Arrow Team Leader; Ray T. Capp, Vice Chairman, Technology and Special Projects; Jack S. Butler II, Vice Chairman, Communications & Marketing; Craig B Salazar; Marty Tschetter; Kenneth P. Davis, PhD.; Edward A. Pease, Past Chairman, National Order of the Arrow Committee; David C. Dowty, Director, *ArrowCorps*[5] Instructor Corps; and Ian Romaine.

Special thanks go to all five of the Incident Commanders: Matthew W. Walker, John W. Hess, L. Ronald Bell, Steven D. Bradley, and Daniel T. Segersin, who are all members of the National Order of the Arrow Committee, for their detailed research and records provided from each site, and to Tim Beaty, National Partnership Coordinator, U.S. Forest Service, for the material furnished from the U.S. Forest Service and for his wise counsel and guidance during the entire project. We are also grateful to Marc Reyes, The Idea Farm, for the creative graphic design layout of the book and his dedication to our project. Finally, special acknowledgement goes to Elizabeth Rouse Fielder, a Chapter Adviser and Brotherhood member for her hours of detailed editing, critiques, and guidance rendered in the preparation of this commemorative book. Lastly, I am grateful to the National Order of the Arrow Committee for the privilege to serve and for their confidence in the *ArrowCorps*[5] Commemorative Photo Book Project.

Thomas E. Fielder
Adviser, *ArrowCorps*[5] Digital Media Team
National Order of the Arrow Committee

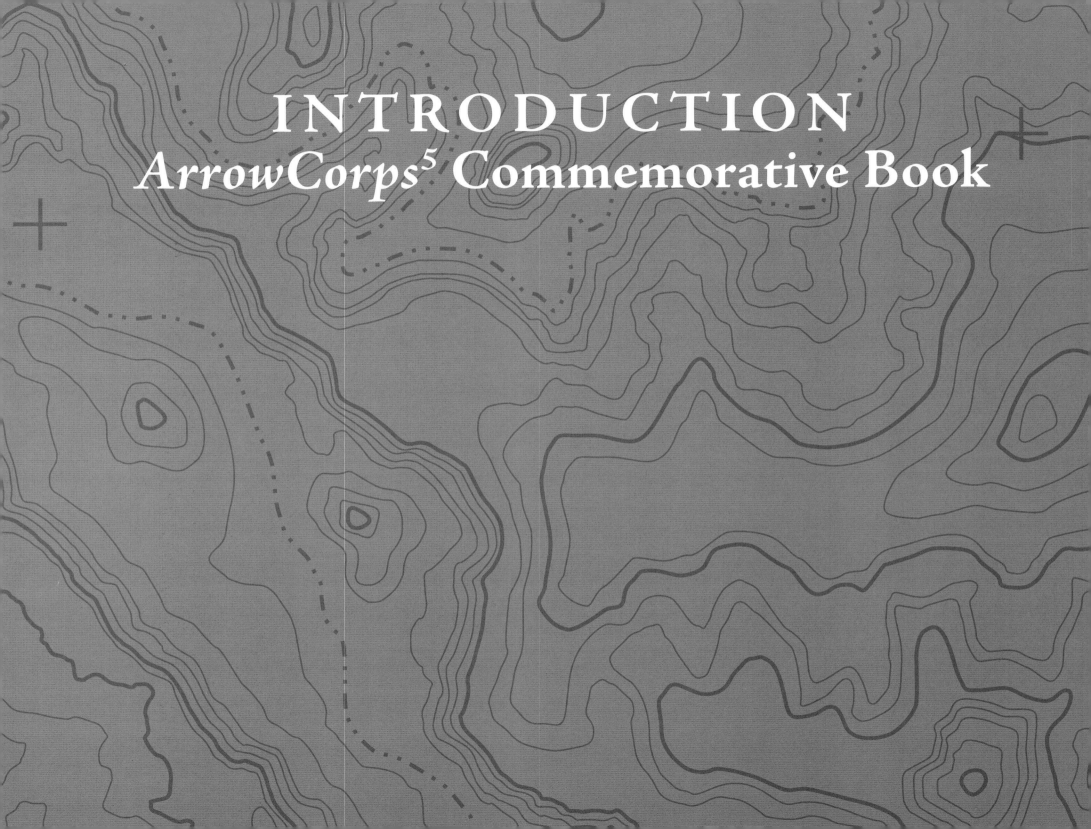

INTRODUCTION
ArrowCorps⁵ Commemorative Book

Sometime late in 2003, we began exploring opportunities to expand the Order of the Arrow's relationship with the United States Forest Service. Our shared vision was to identify and develop effective ways to set a positive example and publicly demonstrate the meaning of leadership in service. Today, one year after completion of the *ArrowCorps⁵* project, as I reflect on those initial discussions, I am reminded of our own beginnings as Scouting's national honor society.

In the fledgling years of Scouting, a young camp director and his assistant searched for a meaningful way to recognize those Scouts in camp who best exemplified the Scout Oath and Scout Law in their daily lives. Ninety-four years ago they found it at a small camp called Treasure Island.

It was a simple idea! Reinforce and instill the values of Scouting by example. Encourage brotherhood, cheerfulness, and service through ceremony and tradition. In their early twenties at the time, E. Urner Goodman and Carroll A. Edson could only hope, but surely could not have imagined, that their simple idea would have such a significant and profound effect on Scouting and each of us personally.

Similarly, more than a decade ago, the Order of the Arrow embarked on a small experimental program at Philmont Scout Ranch called the OA Trail Crew. This highly successful program began because a young section chief believed we could serve our national high adventure bases by building and repairing trails in the backcountry. Little did he or anyone else know at the time that the next 14 years would see the successful growth and development of the OA Trail Crew program, and the introduction and further success of the OA Wilderness Voyage at the Northern Tier High Adventure Bases in 1999 and the OA Outdoor Adventure at the Florida Sea Base in 2005.

Recognition of the Order of the Arrow's service in the Boundary Waters Canoe Area Wilderness in northern Minnesota by the U.S. Forest Service in 2003 with the Chief's Volunteer Award for Youth Service led to those discussions mentioned earlier. Seeing a unique opportunity to provide an even higher level of service during the summer of 2008, we chose to undertake an unprecedented national service project focusing on conservation, environmental sustainability, and wildlife habitat benefits. Over time, we narrowed down the U.S. Forest Service's suggested list of

national forests to five sites. Soon, thereafter, the *ArrowCorps⁵* project was born and planning began.

The Boy Scouts of America's theme for 2008 was the Year of the Volunteer. Through the efforts and teamwork of Arrowmen literally from around the world, Scouting showcased last summer what youth and adult volunteers focused on a common objective can accomplish in just a few short weeks. *ArrowCorps⁵* served to highlight and reinforce Scouting's commitment to service. Its success demonstrated something much more – that Scouting's volunteers are looking for and will positively respond to meaningful opportunities to serve others.

The *ArrowCorps⁵* project was the largest service project undertaken by the Boy Scouts of America since World War II and the largest single volunteer service project ever received by the U.S. Forest Service in its rich 103 year history. Working in close partnership with the U.S. Forest Service, youth and adult members of the Order of the Arrow provided more than 280,000 man-hours of service to our nation's forests, worth approximately $5.6 million.

It was a privilege for me to participate in and visit each of the five *ArrowCorps⁵* project sites. The greatest privilege, however, was the opportunity to meet, talk to, and work with participants and staff. In each one I felt and observed their excitement, enthusiasm, and satisfaction as they toiled with one another for something greater than themselves. Theirs was a renewed sense of pride and purpose. Universally, participants would ask me *"Why haven't we done this before?"* and *"When are we going to do this again?"*

Surprisingly, most also commented that it was the best Boy Scout event in which they had ever participated, including National and World Jamborees, National Order of the Arrow Conferences, and high adventure programs. Why? Because the true impact of the project was in the life-changing experience gained as they served. Shortly before I left for the fifth and final project site last summer, a handwritten note arrived from Ed Pease, my predecessor, who summed up the essence of *ArrowCorps⁵* as only he can. Ed observed that *". . . it has been transformational for the OA – not just because others now see us differently, but because we see ourselves differently, too."*

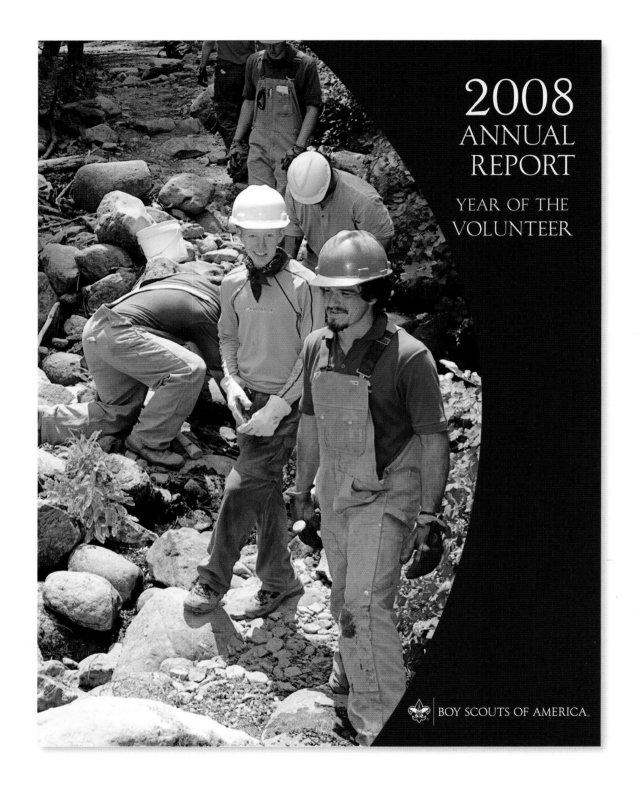

2008
ANNUAL
REPORT

YEAR OF THE
VOLUNTEER

BOY SCOUTS OF AMERICA

The *ArrowCorps5* project was prominently featured in the Boy Scouts of America's 2008 Annual Report distributed at the annual meeting in May and the Order of the Arrow was recognized by the BSA during the meeting with the prestigious William T. Hornaday Gold Certificate. The William T. Hornaday Gold Certificate is granted to organizations or individuals by the National Council of the Boy Scouts of America for demonstrated leadership and commitment to environmental and conservation education of youth on a regional, national, or international level over a minimum period of three years.

During the planning and development of the project we hoped it would inspire participants to internalize the values of initiative, fellowship, teamwork, and servant leadership, to take home those lessons learned through hard work and example, and to eagerly apply those values and lessons at home in service to their council, community, and country. We are convinced that it did just that!

No matter whether you were an *ArrowCorps5* participant, a staff member, or a dedicated U.S. Forest Service professional, we trust these pages and the video bring back fond memories of your involvement in *ArrowCorps5*. If you were a sponsor, we believe you will take great pride in knowing you played a significant part in the success of the project. Finally, if this is your first time with us along the trail, we hope you sense the adventure, fellowship, hard work, dedication, fun, and pride that transformed each of us last summer as we lost ourselves in service to others.

Bradley E. Haddock
Chairman, National Order of the Arrow Committee

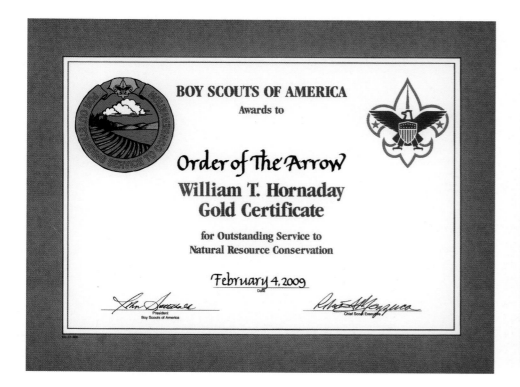

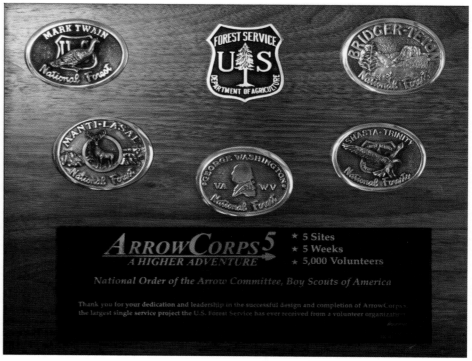

CHAPTER I
A BRIEF HISTORY OF THE ORDER OF THE ARROW

In 1915, just five years after the founding of the Boy Scouts of America (BSA), two 24 year old Scouting professionals in Philadelphia, E. Urner Goodman and Carroll A. Edson, were asked to run a summer camp program at Treasure Island Scout Camp on a small island in the Delaware River. They developed a Camp Honor Society that would celebrate those Scouts in each Troop who represented the best of the Scout Oath and Law, as chosen by their fellow Scouts. Each newly elected candidate would be put through a ceremony to join the "Wimachtendienk," a brotherhood whose traditions and beliefs are loosely based on the legends and stories of the Delaware Indians, or the Lenni Lenape. The honor society legend told about Chief Chingachgook and his son, Uncas, who searched among the various villages of the tribe to find those who would be willing to confront a warlike tribe threatening the homeland. After the selected ones succeeded and defeated the "fierce marauders," they were "bound together in a great and honored order" that devoted their lives to serving others.

On July 16, 1915, based on this legend the first ceremony took place at Treasure Island inducting two members who were led to a campfire area where they faced three tests. First, they tried to encircle a great tree with their arms, but could not do so without the help from other members. Second, they were asked to place twigs on the fire to increase its light; and third, they were required to climb a steep hill that could not be accomplished without the help of their brothers. These three tests were symbolic of Brotherhood, Cheerfulness and Service which were embodied in the Lenni Lenape words of "Wimichtendienk, Wingolauchsik, Witahemui." The abbreviation quickly became "The WWW Society," and, in the beginning, only members knew the meaning of the words. Later, the first Order of the Arrow lodge, Unami, was formed at Treasure Island along with a more structured "Ordeal."

Dr. Goodman speaking to early campfire

Since that time, the Ordeal has evolved into a four-fold test, carried out in a 24 hour period where each candidate must: sleep alone under the stars, to indicate their bravery and camping skills; carry out arduous labor, "more or less distasteful" during the daylight hours to show their commitment to service; eat "scant" food to show their ability to deny themselves for others; and, maintain silence for the entire period, to "turn their thoughts inward" and reflect on the meaning of the experience. The arrow was chosen as the symbol of the society's focus on an upward path in life, shown as a white sash embroidered with a red arrow pointing upward, worn over the right shoulder of members. Members referred to "The WWW Society" while the outside world knew the group as "The Order of the Arrow (OA)."

Unami Lodge was the first lodge, followed by the founding of a second lodge at another council's camp. By 1921, lodges had formed in Maryland, New Jersey, and Pennsylvania, and a Grand Lodge of the Order of the Arrow was created as a "national" organization to oversee the OA. Urner Goodman was elected as the first National Chief; and a Purpose of the Order was written in four parts that still governs today:

To recognize those campers—Scouts and Scouters—who best exemplify the Scout Oath in their daily lives and by such recognition cause other campers to conduct themselves in a manner as to warrant recognition.

Bradley E. Haddock, 1975-76 National Chief, Order of the Arrow

13

December 1968 OA Planning Meeting. Current National Committee Members Randall Cline, Edward Pease, Past Chairman of the National Committee, and Thomas E. Fielder, 1969 National Conference Chief, are shown in the photo.

To develop and maintain camping traditions and spirit.

To promote Scout camping, which reaches its greatest effectiveness as a part of the unit's camping program, both year-round and in the summer camp, as directed by the camping committee of the council.

To crystallize the Scout habit of helpfulness into a life purpose of leadership in cheerful service to others.

While the purposes of the Order were good, in 1922 several Scout professionals objected to secret societies within the BSA. Then Chief Scout Executive James E. West allowed the OA activities to continue, because they reinforced Scouting principles; however, he asked Goodman and Edson to refrain from recruiting and promoting the Order to other camps.

The Order grew slowly through the 1920s and early 1930s. By 1930, the OA was formally approved as an optional program for local councils. The Great Depression and World War II slowed growth in the Order to a stall. During this time, Scout Executives led the Grand Lodge, just as Urner Goodman envisioned; Carroll Edson later became National Chief; as did Arthur Schuck of Reading, PA; and Joseph A. Brunton of the Pittsburg area (Schuck and Brunton each eventually became Chief Scout Executive). From 1940 to 1946, H. Lloyd Nelson, became the first volunteer to serve as National Chief.

After the War, the OA national level officials became more active and proposed Area Leaders to maintain closer contact with lodges. In the late 1940s, the Grand Lodge authorized each area to elect an Area Conference Chief who would oversee a "Pow Wow" weekend event for area lodges designed for training, fellowship, competition and fun - what we call a Section Conclave. At that time, the Area Conference Chiefs term ended with the Pow Wow; today, the term of Section Chiefs continues throughout the year with added responsibilities.

The BSA continued to focus on ways to provide character building experiences for young men and decided to integrate the OAs outdoor programs into the BSA to be a part of the Camping and Engineering Service. In 1948, at the national OA meeting at Indiana University, all sitting members of the Grand Lodge executive committee became members of the National Order of the Arrow Committee within the BSA. All the records and assets of the OA were taken over by the BSA and the National Director of Camping, Wes Klusmann, assumed responsibility for the OA. Within a year, all professionals who had been Grand Lodge officers left the new committee.

The OA evolved into a youth-empowering organization. In 1948, each functional NOAC committee (shows, training, special events, etc.) was chaired by a member of the Grand Lodge or a national professional Scouter who was paired with a "Junior Chairman," or a youth under 21, who had been active in his lodge and area. Based on the positive experience with the Junior Chairmen, the National OA

Committee decided to allow the youth to lead at the next conference. In 1949, Dick Wilson of Washington, Pennsylvania was elected as the first National Conference Chief and 8 other Area Conference Chiefs became the chairmen of the various committees for NOAC, advised by members of the National OA Committee. This is the model of youth leadership used today. In 1950 at the National Jamboree at Valley Forge, an OA Service Corps was developed that has become an important part of the OAs service to the BSA today.

During the 1950s, the OA continued to grow steadily. Generally, NOAC was held every 2 years, Area Pow Wows continued, and locally, the OA served the council and community providing young men with opportunities to exercise leadership. The OAs 50th Anniversary was celebrated in 1965 at NOAC at Indiana University. During the December, 1968 Planning Meeting, Thomas E. Fielder, an Area Chief who had served as the Senior Patrol Leader of the OA Service Corps for the 1969 International Jamboree at Farragut State Park, Idaho, was elected to serve as the last National *Conference* Chief of the OA . He was subsequently appointed by the President of the BSA to become Scouting's first "Youth" Representative to the National Executive Board of the Boy Scouts of America. The National Conference Chief title then changed to National Chief with the election of Paul Pruitt to the post during the 1970 planning meeting.

In 1974, two decisions were made that helped the OA and the BSA. First, the OA negotiated with national BSA officials to become self-sustaining using funds raised from various resources and agreed to pay the salary and benefits of the BSA National Executive Secretary and staff that helped to administer the OA, while the BSA agreed to pay for the OAs costs for office space, telephone calls and travel. This change ultimately resulted in the creation of the National OA Trust Fund within the BSA Trust Fund to provide scholarships, grants to lodges, awards encouraging camping, and funding to assist Native American scouts to attend summer camp. Secondly, the OA now called for a Region Chief and a Region OA Chairman in each of the six regions of the BSA, providing a clear chain of communications from the local level, through section and region to the national level and back. Within a few years, the OA developed a national training course for lodge officers called the National Leadership Seminar (NLS) that was later revised and has become one of the best youth leader courses available. The BSA

Dr. E. Urner Goodman and Carroll A. Edson

incorporated the revised NLS material into its premier adult training course, called "Wood Badge."

Through the 1980s and 1990s, Vice Chairmen were added to the OA National Committee to oversee the many OA activities, including the expanding role at the National Jamboree. An Indian Village was added demonstrating Indian culture and skills, and the Outdoor Adventure Place was added to allow jamboree scouts to experience new outdoor programs, like COPE confidence courses, and pioneering and cooking schemes. In 1997, an interactive, ethical-learning show was added, similar to NOAC shows. The first jamboree show was called "Odyssey of the Law," followed by "Scoutopia" in 2001 and "Twelve Cubed" in 2005. Each show guides Scouts through difficult situations to help them make ethical choices using the Scout Oath and Law. The OA shows at National Jamborees are directed and staged by the youth and are a big hit with the audience.

Other special OA events have been held over the years including an Indian Pow Wow held at Philmont Scout Ranch, and another one later in Powell, Wyoming. In 2003, an "Indian Summer" event provided special training in Indian culture and ceremonies. Special Philmont Treks have been held in years when the date of the bi-annual NOAC was moved to avoid conflicts with other national BSA events. In 1999, the OA held its first Leadership Summit at Colorado State University where the first OA Strategic Plan was developed.

In the 1990s, the OA focused on providing service in camping areas by teaching Arrowmen the skills they needed to manually improve outdoor properties. The first product of this focus was the OA Trail Crew program in the 137,000 acres of Rocky Mountain wilderness at Philmont Scout Ranch. The program would provide needed conservation-centered improvements at Philmont and a re-commitment to the OA purposes of Brotherhood, Cheerfulness and Service by Arrowmen. Trail Crew at Philmont started in 1995 with Scout groups of 10 selected from applicants all over

Dr. Goodman at the closing of the 1969 National Order of the Arrow Conference with Thomas E. Fielder, 1969 National Conference Chief and first Youth Representative to the National Executive Board Boy Scouts of America

the country. A week of trail work was scheduled, followed by a week of backpacking. The modest fee of $100 plus transportation opened the door to more Arrowmen from all areas. Ceremonies and discussions on ethical principles were developed that focused on OA purposes and principles during the event.

Based upon the success of Philmont Trail Crew, in 1999 the OA decided to offer a similar program improving the portages at the BSA's Northern Tier High Adventure Base outside Ely, Minnesota, called "OA Wilderness Voyage." While the BSA's land is relatively small at Northern Tier, it sits next to the 1.2 million acre Boundary Waters Canoe Area Wilderness operated by the U.S. Forest Service. The U.S. Forest Service granted permission to the OA to access the national forest lands and each spring its local personnel trains the OA staff in the proper techniques. Regular visits to the portage sites allowed the Forest Service to monitor work practices and progress in the Boundary Waters. Since its beginning, the program quickly became a success and earned the respect of the U.S. Forest Service leadership. Like the Philmont Trail Crew program, the Wilderness Voyage

program is carried out in the summer with crews of approximately 10 led by a foreman and an assistant during a week of portage improvement work, followed by a week of canoeing wherever the participants want to go. In 2003, the local Forest Service District awarded the OA Wilderness Voyage a top U. S. Forest Service Award for the positive impact the program had on the Boundary Waters area.

From this small success in Minnesota would grow the kernel of an idea about a national OA service project in 2008. This project would be called *ArrowCorps5* and would give exceptional service to five national Forests from Virginia to California. We eagerly await the next chapter in the OAs history of servant leadership.

This chapter is based on history compiled by Kenneth P. Davis, PhD., Ed Pease, and Robert Mason. For more information see: *Brotherhood of Cheerful Service: A History of the Order of the Arrow* by: Kenneth P. Davis, PhD.

2008 National Chief Jake Wellman (right) and 2008 National Vice Chief Ben Stilwill shown at the Manti-La Sal site.

2008 National Order of the Arrow Committee

Jacob P. Wellman (Y)
National Chief

Benjamin L. Stilwill (Y)
National Vice Chief

S. Tyler Elliott (Y)
Region Chief

Mark P. Hendricks (Y)
Region Chief

Patrick W. Rooney (Y)
Region Chief

J. Mason Thomas (Y)
Region Chief

Bradley E. Haddock
National Chairman

Clyde M. Mayer (P)
OA Team Leader

Carey L. Miller (P)
OA Specialist

Glenn T. Ault
Vice Chairman
Financial Resources

L. Ronald Bell
Vice Chairman
Recognition and Awards

Jack S. Butler, II
Vice Chairman
Communications and
Marketing

Ray T. Capp
Vice Chairman
Technology and Special
Projects

Mark J. Chilutti
Vice Chairman
Leadership Development

John W. Hess
Vice Chairman
Lodge Operations

Michael G. Hoffman
Vice Chairman
National Events

Carl M. Marchetti
Vice Chairman
Founders Council

Thomas E. Reddin
Vice Chairman
Region and Section
Operations

Daniel T. Segersin
Vice Chairman
Outdoor Program

James R. Barbieri
Scott W. Beckett
Michael D. Bliss
Forrest L. Bolles
Steven D. Bradley
Toby D. Capps
Evan P. Chaffee (Y)
Randall K. Cline
Wayne L. Dukes
Thomas E. Fielder
Douglas C. Fullman (P)
Christopher A. Grove
Daniel W. Hayes (P)
J. Terry Honan
Jason P. Hood
Jeffery Q. Jonasen
William D. Loeble

J. Dan McCarthy
Dan McDonough, Jr.
Carey J. Mignerey
Ryan R. Miske
Larry M. Newton (Y)
Edward A. Pease
Hector A. "Tico" Perez
Bruce A. Sanders
Max Sasseen, Jr.
Eugene J. Schnell
Robert J. Sirhal
N. Anthony Steinhardt, III
Jeffery C. Stout (P)
W. Keith Swedenburg (P)
Clint E. Takeshita
Michael L. Thompson
Kaylene D. Trick

John T. Van Dreese (P)
P. Eugene Wadford
Matthew M. Walker
Billy W. Walley

FOUNDERS COUNCIL
Kenneth P. Davis
Esten F. Grubb
Dabney Kennedy
Delbert W. Loder
James W. Palmer, Jr.
James H. Simpson

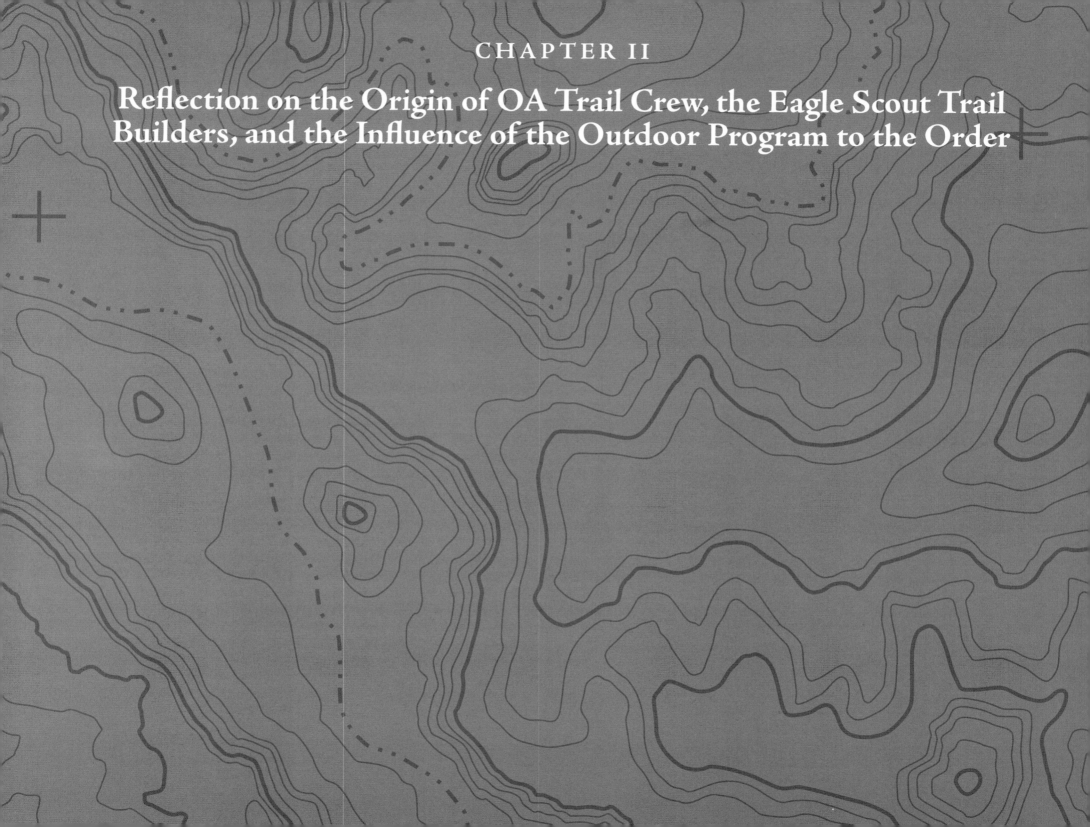

CHAPTER II

Reflection on the Origin of OA Trail Crew, the Eagle Scout Trail Builders, and the Influence of the Outdoor Program to the Order

The power of the outdoors is humbling; the grandeur speaks to the soul. It is a neutral classroom that strengthens inner-reflection, self-reliance, renews a spirit of commitment to service, and can generate positive growth. Perpetually important to the Order, the outdoors has always been important to Scouting.

When the Boy Scouts of America was only thirteen years old, Edgar Maclay, then president of the North Central Montana Council in Great Falls, Montana, proposed to the National Park Service an elegant idea *"whereby boys who have attained the rank of Eagle Scout shall be permitted to give of themselves and their services toward the development of our nationwide playground system. The strong point that I am endeavoring to develop is the spirit of service amongst boys. I believe that the amount of service that they can be inspired to render will be a measure of the fullness of their citizenship."*

The ambitious proposal was mailed to the Director of the National Park Service Stephen Mather and the local Representative in Congress, the Honorable Scott Leavitt. Over the course of the next twenty-one months, meetings were held and ideas exchanged through letters of correspondence between government and Scouting officials. The proposal was accepted; next promotion of the event and logistics had to be planned. The National Park Service selected the project, agreed to furnish personnel to direct and supervise the youth, and provide food. The former Region 11 Boy Scout office, which covered Montana, Idaho, Washington, and Oregon, agreed to provide professional staff to serve as the lead directors. And the Great Northern Railroad transported participants from the park entrance to the work site.

Eagle Scouts were selected on account of the anticipated 'hard work' and because the Eagle Scout Trail offered a new incentive for keeping advanced Scouts in the program. The trail building projects offered all the romance of camping 'out West,' the opportunity to carry out the daily 'good turn,' and to explore the local terrain.

Yellowstone National Park hosted the first project in 1925, then subsequent projects were held in Glacier, Yosemite, Mount Rainier, and Crater Lake National Parks. The Glacier projects continued the longest, through 1934, though eventually ended by the economic constraints of the Great Depression. Originally promoted to Scouts from Oregon, Washington, Idaho, and Montana, by the end, Scouts as far away as Minnesota, Pennsylvania, Vermont, Virginia, Tennessee, and Alabama participated. Some traveled by bicycle, a few hitchhiked, but most came by train. All made the trip to perform unselfish service.

The projects lasted two weeks. New trail was constructed in the morning followed by hiking and nature talks in the afternoon. In the evening, after dinner, they had rousing campfires and dreamed about their futures. The last night was spent on the Blackfeet Indian Reservation, where one of the Scouts – duly elected by his fellows – was an honorary inductee into the tribe.

The Order of the Arrow Trail Crew was launched during the summer of 1995, the Order of the Arrow's national "year of service." The program was the outgrowth of a vision by a section chief, who happened to also be serving as a Philmont Ranger. This youth officer felt that the ORDER OF THE ARROW could benefit from an outdoor program to reinforce camping methods, self-reliance, further develop leadership, provide a tangible service project, and in general to provide youth an opportunity to experience a true adventure of the spirit. The influence of just how important this young man's vision was, as 'the power of one,' is a testament to the spirit of Scouting.

The Order of the Arrow set out to build a trail at Philmont and create a unique outdoor education program designed for youth by youth. This new venture was a perfect fit at the time for the Order of the Arrow, causing the 'honor campers' of Scouting to search within themselves. Originally slated for one year, the success was overwhelming and the National OA Committee and Philmont management decided to continue the program and complete the first trail that was started. After the first trail was completed, a second key decision was made to continue the OA Trail Crew program through subsequent summers.

1931 Eagle Scout Trail Builders

2008 *ArrowCorps*[5] **– Bridger-Teton**

1931 Eagle Scout Trail Builder

2008 *ArrowCorps Loop* **– George Washington & Jefferson**

By 1999 a similar program had expanded to Northern Tier National High Adventure Base. Deep in the wilds of the Minnesota Boundary Waters Canoe Area Wilderness, the Order of the Arrow Wilderness Voyage matured through paddle, canoe, solace, and improved portage passages. The U.S. Forest Service managed the vast boundary waters territory and over time a healthy partnership grew with the Order. Only four years after its inception, the U.S. Forest Service recognized the OA Voyage program in 2003 with their prestigious Chief's Volunteer Award for Youth Volunteer Service. The nomination prominently cited the program's impact, "For the past four years your organization has recruited, trained, and lead the work of hundreds of enthusiastic volunteers. The quality and quantity of work accomplished was exceptional. Miles of portages were improved using primitive tools and a great deal of physical effort. The wilderness experience of thousands of visitors for many years to come will be enhanced due to your efforts to protect our valuable wilderness resources."

Another milestone achieved in 2005 was the launching of the Ocean Adventure at the Florida Sea Base. The proven success of all three national OA youth high adventure programs and the strong relationship with the U.S. Forest Service from the OA Voyage, collectively served as a direct catalyst to seek "a higher adventure," which became *ArrowCorps*[5].

The legacy of the high adventure program to the Order is the values learned. Youth have sought a romantic quest for experience by traveling across our nation to remote wilderness areas to provide cheerful service. The programs experienced through the outdoors bring to life the tenets of the Order: brotherhood through camaraderie, cheerfulness through a positive attitude, and service by a tangible project. Cut from the same bolt of cloth, there is a strong parallel to Maclay's vision more than eighty years ago, that "the American boy will respond in an inspiring way if given the opportunity."

After the 1928 Eagle Scout Trail Building project at Glacier National Park, assistant director Ronald Ruddiman from Seattle wrote in his diary, "I believe that the experience that these boys enjoyed here is one that will benefit them in many ways. They will have seen a wonderful section of our great mountain country, will have enjoyed new friendships from far parts of the United States, will have appreciated what it means to perform real physical labor, and to cut a trail through the wilderness."

A hallmark of Scouting is the timelessness of values, even generations apart. The same enthusiasm, motivation, pursuit of adventure, nearly one hundred years later demonstrate that truly the "ideals remain the same." The richness of Scouting comes to life through strong outdoor program.

Marty Tschetter

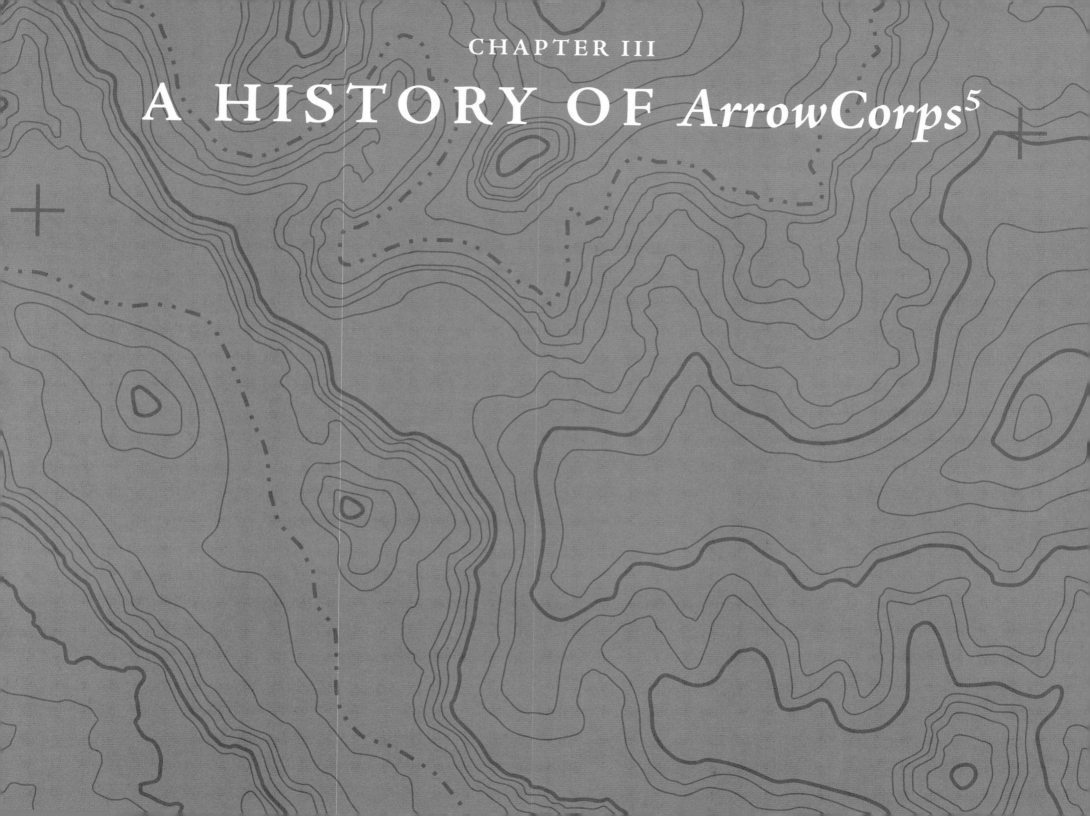

CHAPTER III
A HISTORY OF *ArrowCorps⁵*

Laying the Groundwork

ArrowCorps[5] was built on the Order of the Arrow's rich heritage of service to local council programs, facilities, and camps, and the success of its service to the Boy Scouts of America's high adventure bases. Following the launch of OA Trail Crew – the OA's first high adventure program – in 1995 at Philmont Scout Ranch, the OA continued to expand its national leadership and service programs with the addition of OA Wilderness Voyage at the Northern Tier High Adventure Bases in 1999, and the OA Ocean Adventure at the Florida Sea Base in 2005. The U.S. Forest Service presented the OA with the Chief's Volunteer Award for Youth Volunteer Service in 2003, its highest volunteerism award, for the OA's *"exemplary service and efforts"* in the Boundary Waters Canoe Area Wilderness in northern Minnesota.

In anticipation of Scouting's 100th anniversary, the Boy Scouts of America moved the National Jamboree to 2010 instead of the normal four-year cycle that would have scheduled the next Jamboree in 2009. Looking forward, the Order of the Arrow was able to adjust its biennial National Order of the Arrow Conference schedule, pushing the 2008 conference to 2009. With the move from even to odd years, the Order of the Arrow is poised to hold a gala conference to celebrate its centennial anniversary in 2015. These changes allowed us to explore opportunities to expand the OA's relationship with the U.S. Forest Service.

Ed Pease, past chairman of the National Order of the Arrow Committee, and Clyde Mayer, Director of the Order of the Arrow, met in June 2003, with Mark Rey, Under Secretary for Natural Resources and Environment, U.S. Department of Agriculture, and Dale Bosworth, Chief of the U.S. Forest Service, to discuss the possibility of conducting a significant conservation project for the U.S. Forest Service in 2008. Mark Rey, an Eagle Scout and Vigil Honor member, and Chief Bosworth endorsed the concept, indicating it was consistent with the Chief's newly launched campaign entitled *"More Kids in the Woods."* The 2008 national conservation service project was discussed in concept by the National Order of the Arrow Committee at the December 2003 planning meeting.

In March 2004, Tim Beaty, National Partnership Coordinator for Senior, Youth, and Volunteer Programs with the U.S. Forest Service, notified every Forest Supervisor in the United States that a national conservation service project was being considered for the summer of 2008. Each Forest Supervisor was asked if they had any projects that would require 800 to 1000 Boy Scouts and adult leaders to complete and the project could wait until 2008. Of the 155 Forests across the United States, 13 Forests identified projects for consideration.

Working together, criteria were developed to identify public lands that would most benefit from a massive volunteer service initiative consistent with the type of work performed at existing Order of the Arrow high adventure programs. Criteria focused on four main threats identified by the U.S. Forest Service – fire and fuel reduction, invasive species, loss of open spaces, and unmanaged outdoor recreation. Consideration was also given to the uniqueness of the project, ability to impact the Forest area, ability to support the project logistically and financially, project marketability, proximity to the four BSA regions, and whether the scope of each project was something that could be accomplished during a one week period.

During a meeting held on April 3, 2004, in Ogden, Utah, five sites were jointly selected based on these needs and priorities, and the OA's ability to provide the type of service required at each site. The five sites selected were Mark Twain in Missouri, Manti-La Sal in Utah, George Washington & Jefferson in Virginia, Shasta-Trinity in California, and Bridger-Teton in Wyoming. The once simple concept of a national service project that we thought would be conducted at a single site had quickly become a major logistical undertaking to be conducted at five disparate locations scattered across the country. The proposed 2008 national service project was approved by the National Order of the Arrow Committee at its meeting on May 19, 2004, during the annual national meetings of the Boy Scouts of America in Chicago, Illinois.

By the December 2004 planning meeting, the lead advisers for each project site had been appointed – Dan Segersin, Eden Prairie, Minnesota, would serve at Bridger-Teton; Ron Bell, Miami, Florida, would serve at George Washington & Jefferson; Jack Hess, Lafayette, Colorado, would serve at Manti-La Sal; Matt Walker, Richardson, Texas, would serve at Mark Twain; and, Steve Bradley, Riverside, California, would serve at Shasta-Trinity. The first organizational meeting was held on December 29, 2004. Each lead adviser was an experienced member of the National OA Committee. The meeting agenda included a lengthy list of daunting issues ranging from organizational structure and staff recruitment, youth leadership roles, naming of the project, incident command training requirements and schedule, site visit schedule, minimum age and physical requirements, staffing needs and schedule for OA Trail Crew, OA Wilderness Voyage, and OA Outdoor Adventure during 2008, commercial sponsors, and project promotion and marketing.

What's an Incident Commander?

Because the Order of the Arrow would be teaming with the U.S. Forest Service at each site, the Incident Command System or ICS, used by most federal, state, and local agencies to respond to emergencies was adopted. This management system is a flexible, scalable response organization that provides a common framework within which people can work together effectively. The OA and the U.S. Forest Service would each appoint an Incident Commander for each site and the framework which is normally used to respond to emergencies would be implemented to plan and execute the work at every site. The OA's five lead advisers became known as Incident Commanders and key leadership had to be trained in the Incident Command System. Understanding and adapting to the ICS also meant learning new terms and matching each new phrase with the OA's organizational structure and unique terminology. For example, an ICS "section chief" is not the same thing as a section chief in the OA. The incident command structure has four sections – operations, planning, logistics, and finance/administration. Each section leader is known as a section chief. In any event, we had a lot to learn.

Special guests Smokey Bear and Woodsy Owl along with Brad Haddock, National Chairman; Benjamin Stilwell, 2008 National Vice Chief; and, Jacob (Jake) Wellman, 2008 National Chief

More Planning and Training

During the planning meeting it was decided that the OA leadership summit scheduled for 2007 would serve dual purposes – first, to introduce the OA's new strategic plan and second, to train youth and adults for leadership roles in the 2008 project. Site visits were to be completed by the meeting to be held the following summer at the National Jamboree. Importantly, too, a name for the project had to be developed and would soon be required to begin promotion of the event. Following the meeting, I asked Patrick Murphy, National Chief, and Seth Mollitt, National Vice Chief, to lead the effort to develop a catchy name for the 2008 national service project.

The project leadership team met on July 27, 2005, in Fredericksburg, Virginia, during the National Jamboree. Key agenda items included site visit reports with an explanation of the proposed work projects for each site; Incident Command System training requirements and scheduling; the establishment of the dates for each project site; staff recruiting; identification of common resources and tools that could be shared among the sites; health and safety training and personal protection equipment requirements; OA high adventure program issues; appropriate roles for youth leadership; and, the budget.

"Man Scouts"

During the meeting, it was reported that during a site visit in April, a District Ranger asked what type of projects the OA actually thought it could accomplish at the site. From the question and ensuing discussion it quickly became obvious the Ranger was envisioning a group of very young Boy Scouts or even a den of Cub Scouts out for an afternoon stroll in the woods. Once the type of work done at Philmont and Northern Tier was described, she nodded with approval, and said, "Oh, so, you'll be bringing Man Scouts." Ron Bell, Clyde Mayer, and I agreed. Three years later, following the Friday night gathering at George Washington & Jefferson, the District Ranger made a point to come by to offer her congratulations to Ron Bell and me on having clearly exceeded expectations. As she shook my hand, she smiled and said, "Yes, you were right, they were all 'Man Scouts.'"

Five Weeks, Five Sites, Five Thousand Arrowmen

By the end of the meeting in Fredericksburg, we had settled on the order of and tentative dates for each project site after consideration of the location, relative temperature and humidity, flying pests, and recommendations from local Forest Service personnel. The rotation would be Mark Twain, Manti-La Sal, and George Washington & Jefferson in June, and Shasta-Trinity and Bridger-Teton, with their higher elevations, beginning in the middle of July and possibly stretching into early August. We also agreed the OA Trail Crew, OA Wilderness Voyage, and OA Outdoor Adventure programs should continue through the summer of 2008 after concluding the national service project would complement the three high adventure programs and vice-versa, rather than detract; and that we would lose considerable momentum at the high adventure bases if the programs were suspended for the summer.

Unlike other national OA high adventure programs limited only to youth participation, the national service project provided a unique opportunity for adults to take an active role in meaningful service at each site. For many years, adult Arrowmen had expressed a strong interest in participating in OA Trail Crew at Philmont Scout Ranch and OA Wilderness Voyage at the Northern Tier bases. During the meeting we concluded that youth and adult Arrowmen who met the Philmont height and weight guidelines and completed a BSA Class III physical could participate. Youth participants would be required to be 14 years old by June 1, 2008.

The leadership team also concluded that each site would use the same program, opening and closing gathering scripts, and follow the same basic schedule – participants would arrive on Saturday; crew assignments, tool use and safety training, and the opening gathering would occur on Sunday; fieldwork would be conducted Monday through mid-day on Friday; one day of recreation would be provided for all participants during the week; the closing gathering would be on Friday night; and, all would depart on Saturday morning. Overall, planning was going well. On a worrisome note, however, we had no sponsors and left the meeting without a budget.

What's In a Name?

Meanwhile, the youth officers continued to brainstorm and suggest names for the national service project, but nothing was very catchy or exciting. The leading contenders by July 1, 2005, were *"Arrowmen in Action," "Arrowmen in Service,"* and *"Leaders in Service."* Recognizing our work would span five weeks and five sites, and that plans now called for up to 1000 staff and participants at each site, we began using the phrase *"Five Weeks, Five Sites, Five Thousand Arrowmen"* as shorthand. But, the name continued to elude us.

During a conference call one afternoon in early September, several key words and phrases were thrown out to stimulate discussion – words like *"Service," "Conservation Corps," "Arrowmen,"* and *"Leadership."* The old Civilian Conservation Corps (or "CCC") from the 1930s had been suggested as a starting point several months before. The phrase *"Arrowmen Conservation Corps"* with a numeric superscript five and the initials "ACC" or "ACC 5" had also been suggested to me by Jack Butler, Vice Chairman of the National OA Committee for Communications and Marketing. Finally, without much thought, I observed that a corps of Arrowmen would be

required to accomplish the work planned at each of the five sites. As I heard the words expressed out loud, it occurred to me, it's an Arrowman's corps at five sites – *"Oh!"* I exclaimed, *"How about Arrow Corps Five?"* With a little work, it soon became *ArrowCorps[5]*. We later began using "AC5" internally to refer to the project.

With the project name in hand, a full color brochure describing the *ArrowCorps[5]* project was developed, along with a companion PowerPoint presentation, to introduce the project at the December 2005 planning meeting. These materials were also designed to be used at the 2006 National Order of the Arrow Conference to be held at Michigan State University. The brochure was the first of two brochures published to promote *ArrowCorps[5]*. A promotional patch was distributed at the conference and a limited number of T-shirts were also available.

ICS Training

Working closely with Tim Beaty, we were able to reduce the amount of time required for the Incident Command System training. John E. Roberts, a former career employee of the U.S. Forest Service with extensive experience as a National Incident Command Team member and past director of the federal government's National Interagency Center specializing in Incident Command System training, was selected as the instructor for a specially designed ICS course to be conducted on Saturday and Sunday, February 4 to 5, 2006, at the BSA Center for Professional Development in Westlake, Texas. To condense the ICS training into two days, the 23 individuals attending the training were required to successfully complete the ICS 100 and 200 courses, available on the Internet, and to bring copies of their completion certificates for each course to the training session. John was an excellent instructor. We all left with a solid grasp of the Incident Command System and how it would be used in partnership with the U.S. Forest Service to assure the success and safety of *ArrowCorps[5]*.

It was clear from the outset that "safety first" was a given. The U.S. Forest Service and BSA both place a strong emphasis and high value on safety and training. Safety officers were recruited for each project site. These volunteers worked hand-in-glove with their Forest Service counterparts during the planning stages and throughout each project to assure the health and safety of every participant and staff member, resulting in no serious injuries at any of the sites, only minor scratches and bruises.

Instructor Corps

The ICS training highlighted the need for consistent, qualified leadership at the crew and squad level. This was critical to assure the actual work was performed safely and properly. Based on crew and squad sizes, it was estimated we would need a minimum of 35 experienced crew leaders to assure the success of the work planned for each

site. Rather than try to find, recruit, and train 175 volunteers, it became obvious to the leadership team that we should hire 35 qualified crew leaders. Fortunately, the OA's high adventure programs had been producing directors and trail crew foremen for more than 10 years and these young men would be ideally suited to serve as crew leaders for *ArrowCorps5*.

Of course, the decision to hire crew leaders and form the *Instructor Corps* meant we would have to figure out how to pay, house, feed, and transport the group throughout the summer. Although this was the largest single cost in the *ArrowCorps5* it proved one of the wisest decisions made during the five year planning process. Philmont Scout Ranch offered to serve as the employer and base for the *Instructor Corps* members, and agreed to share the costs of the *Instructor Corps* while they were working at Philmont. This partnership allowed the OA to offer employment to the members for the entire summer and provided an opportunity for them to work together at Philmont when not serving at one of the project sites. David Dowty, a former National Vice Chief and OATC foreman, was hired to serve as the *Instructor Corps* Director and given the responsibility to hire the members of the *Instructor Corps* by the December 2006 planning meeting.

Transportation for the *Instructor Corps* presented a significant challenge because of the disparate Forest locations and the back-to-back scheduling of the first three projects. Planes, trains, and buses were considered. Only air transportation would work. Commercial air travel was "out" for a group of 42 with extensive luggage and tools. After all, how do you explain a personalized Pulaski to a TSA agent as you work your way through the line at the airport? The only workable answer was to charter a 50-passenger jet. With the help of Larry Kellner, an Eagle Scout, National Executive Board member, and the Chairman and CEO of Continental Airlines, the OA was introduced to Rick Croasdale, a former Cub Scout and the Aviation Director at ExpressJet Corporate Aviation. Rick worked diligently on the *Instructor*

Corps itinerary and provided a significant discount, until we had the first chartered airplane in the history of the BSA, an EMB-145XR, soon to be known as *ICorps One*.

Digital Media Team and the Photo Contest

Led by the creative energy from Robert Mason, an OA Section Chief, and Terrel Miller, a dedicated adult volunteer, we decided to assemble a Digital Media Team to preserve the project in words, photographs, and video. Robert Mason was hired as a member of the *Instructor Corps* and served as the Youth Coordinator of digital images for the team. Terrel Miller, with his extensive professional credentials and years of experience with BSA and OA shows, generously volunteered his time to serve as the team's videographer. Thomas E. Fielder, a member of the National OA Committee volunteered to serve as the Adviser of the newly created Digital Media Team and the coordinator of the Photo Contest described below. Robert and Terrel traveled throughout the summer with the *Instructor Corps* and captured most of the wonderful photographs and video included in this book and accompanying DVD. In addition to photographing the sites, Robert also collected digital photos from dozens of other Arrowmen serving *ArrowCorps5* at all five sites.

After having made the commitment to the collection of digital media from the sites, we decided to encourage all participants to contribute to the collection of historical images of the work through a Photo Contest. The Photo Contest was divided into youth and adult categories for each site. Contestants entered the contest through an inter-active upload connection on the OA *ArrowCorps5* web site. We received 157 entries. At the December 2008 planning meeting, the Section Chiefs viewed all 158 entries and selected the winners for each category. The winning entries from the photo contest along with digital images collected from the participants formed the backbone for this book. First priority for selection of photographs was given to the

winning photos from the photo contest, followed by images provided by the youth *ArrowCorps⁵* participants, and then photos from the Digital Media Team.

Budgets

As a result of additional site visits and input from Forest personnel, preliminary budgets were developed for each project site by the Incident Commanders and Clyde Mayer. These budgets were combined with the project management budget resulting in estimated expenses of just under $2.5 million for the entire project. We quickly realized that with 5,000 staff and participants, the fee would have to be at least $500 per person. This was simply too much to ask youth and adult Arrowmen, no matter how dedicated, to pay and volunteer to engage in hard physical labor for a week. The leadership team believed the fee should be consistent with a council summer camp fee and agreed to set the fee for *ArrowCorps⁵* at $250 for staff and participants. The decision meant the OA would have to raise $1.25 million in cash, discounts, and in-kind gifts, or look for significant ways to cut expenses, or both.

Promotion, Planning, and Training

ArrowCorps⁵ was heavily promoted at the 2006 National Order of the Arrow Conference held at Michigan State University. In addition, the National Conservation and Leadership Summit ("NCLS") scheduled for the following summer at Indiana University was also promoted. Designed with two distinct tracks, NCLS would, first, introduce the 2008 to 2012 Order of the Arrow Strategic Plan – *Living the Legacy* – to lodge leadership and provide tools for the plan's implementation in the local council; and, second, provide leadership and conservation training, including field training in the Hoosier National Forest, to participants who intended to serve on the *ArrowCorps⁵* staff at one or more of the project sites in 2008.

Following the conference, the leadership team and incident command teams for each site diligently worked to complete a large number of tasks by the December 2006 planning meeting. These items included completion of ICS organizational charts, confirmation of staging areas, completion of needs lists, identification of possible sponsors, completion of the draft budget, identification and description of projects and work plans, development of a robust promotion and recruitment plan for staff and participants, and finalization of the *ArrowCorps⁵* training, including the use of Conservation USA curriculum, to be conducted at the NCLS.

Finding Sponsors

Open issues were brought into sharp focus as 2007 began, especially project finances, staff and participant recruitment, and preparation for the NCLS. In February, Clyde Mayer and I met with James J. Terry, Assistant Chief Scout Executive, and Albert H. Kugler, BSA National Foundation Director, to discuss potential donors and receive advice and approval to approach the donors. Once a list of potential corporate donors was prepared, we worked with the National Foundation to develop a concept paper to be used to explain *ArrowCorps⁵* to potential donors.

The going was tough! By the end of September, we had only received commitments of $100,000 in cash and a number of in-kind contributions totaling $374,000, plus discounts received on the charter, vehicle rentals, and chainsaws. A program pre-proposal was submitted to the National Forest Foundation under their Matching Awards Program requesting $65,000 to support projects in the George Washington & Jefferson National Forests and the Bridger-Teton National Forest. We were notified in January that the proposal was accepted for the full proposal round. The OA had also passed the pre-proposal stage under the National Fish and Wildlife Foundation's Pulling Together Initiative, and was asked to submit a full proposal to the Foundation in January in which we asked for $60,000 in support of the project at Manti-La Sal National Forest. The National Forest Foundation and the National

The December 2007 planning meeting was fast approaching and although we believed at least one of the gifts would be forthcoming, no confirmation had been received. The waiting was agonizing. The National OA Committee meeting scheduled for December 27th was looming. It would either be a celebration or prove a long, difficult meeting of tough decisions about *ArrowCorps*[5].

During the project leadership team meeting held the afternoon before the committee meeting my BlackBerry began to buzz. As though miraculously scripted, it was confirmation of two wire transfers just received by the BSA in the amount of $100,000 and $500,000! Excitement, joy, and relief flooded my emotions as the "monkey" was graciously lifted from my shoulders through the generosity of others. As the announcement was made, everyone in the room breathed a collective sigh of relief. The excitement was palpable. Within the month, a third gift in the amount of $400,000 was received, bringing total cash contributions, including the foundation grants, to more than $1.2 million.

The Big Push

On September 17, 2007, Chief Scout Executive Robert J. Mazzuca, in one of his first communications in his new role, introduced the *ArrowCorps*[5] project to council Scout executives, calling it *"an exciting historical opportunity for the Boy Scouts of America to exercise leadership in service to our nation's forests."* Included was a copy of the reservation information packet encouraging them to *"take an active role in promoting and encouraging your lodge membership to participate in this once-in-a-lifetime event"* that would *"inspire Arrowmen to greater service in your council!"* He noted that:

ArrowCorps[5] *is just the type of creative outdoor program envisioned by our 2006 – 2010 Strategic Plan. As we approach the BSA's 100th anniversary, this project presents a unique opportunity to showcase the timeless values expressed in the Scout Oath and Scout Law, provides greater visibility to our outdoor program and desire to protect the environment, and serves as an excellent starting point as we begin developing collaborative relationships and strategic alliances with other organizations.*

Fish and Wildlife Foundation grants were both received.

With the first project at Mark Twain National Forest less than nine months away, however, it was clear we needed to ask for help and step up the fundraising or be faced with some tough decisions. Fortunately, during the October BSA Executive Board and committee meetings in Dallas, Clyde Mayer and I met with Perry L. Cochell, Senior Endowment Counsel for the BSA National Foundation, to discuss our needs. Perry's belief in the project and commitment to help us succeed was evident and encouraging. Soon after the meeting, Perry called to introduce me to a wonderful Scouter and member of the BSA's Endowment Committee who had agreed to personally ask two individuals for significant cash contributions to *ArrowCorps*[5]. Once he was briefed and received the concept paper and brochures, the presentations were made.

An updated brochure was produced and distributed that included an introductory letter from Bob Mazzuca, updated the project descriptions for each site, confirmed the fee, explained the registration process, and guided prospective staff and participants to the OA's website which provided extensive information about *ArrowCorps5*. Promotional articles were published in the December issue of: *ProSpeak*, a publication for professional scouters; *Boys' Life*, a publication for Boy Scouts; and, *High Country*, the official magazine of the Philmont Staff Association.

Down the Home Stretch

On January 4, 2008, Mike Hoffman, Vice Chairman, National Events; Clyde Mayer; and I held a conference call with Bob Mazzuca; Wayne Brock, Assistant Chief Scout Executive; John Green, Director of Program; George Trosko, Boy Scout Division Director; and Al Kugler, Assistant to the Chief Scout Executive; to update them on the *ArrowCorps5* project. We learned that each member of the CSE leadership team had already checked their calendars and identified which site each one would attend. Bob Mazzuca was scheduled to visit Bridger-Teton and planned to invite President George W. Bush to visit the site while he was there. In addition, Bob Mazzuca agreed to contact key councils to encourage participation and to send out another promotion letter within the next few days to council Scout executives. We agreed to ask each section chief to contact the lodge chiefs because it would be ideal if Bob's letter arrived shortly after the lodge chief was contacted. It was a great way to celebrate a birthday.

The second promotional letter from Bob Mazzuca was mailed on January 15, 2008, to remind Scout executives of the registration deadlines. He also referred to the article in the December issue of *ProSpeak* and encouraged them to become a *Trailblazer Council* in support of *ArrowCorps5*, noting that council leadership would be recognized at the *Trailblazer Council* reception at the 2008 National Annual Meeting in San Diego, California. To qualify, a council had to name youth and adult coordinators, and have a minimum number of members attend *ArrowCorps5*, as a participant or member of the staff, ranging from five to fifty depending on the size of the council.

The 2008 *ArrowCorps5* Service Team Member Emblem was introduced on the Order of the Arrow's website, www.oa-bsa.org, on March 28, 2008, for any Arrowman who had committed to serving on staff or as a participant at one of the sites. The patch was designed to be worn as a temporary patch to promote the event and would be replaced with the arrowhead patch given to each person completing their service at *ArrowCorps5*. In addition to the arrowhead patch, each person would receive a Philmont-style group photograph taken at the site once squad assignments were made.

A meeting with senior leadership of the U.S. Forest Service was held on April 28th in Washington, D.C. Carey Mignerey and Ed Pease attended the meeting on behalf of the National Order of the Arrow Committee. It was evident Forest Service leadership was excited about what had been jointly accomplished and looking forward to the summer. Abigail R. Kimbell, Chief of the U.S. Forest Service, would visit the Bridger-Teton project, and several members of the leadership team planned to visit the other sites. A joint press release from the BSA and U.S. Forest Service was issued the following day announcing the project.

Incident Commander media training was conducted during the May meetings, lead by Stephen Medlicott, BSA Director of Communications and Marketing. The *Trailblazer Council* reception was held on May 21st immediately following the National Order of the Arrow Committee meeting. Ninety-four local councils qualified as Trailblazer Councils and more than 150 people attended the reception, the first reception hosted by the OA at a national annual meeting.

Work that Needed to Be Done

The Forest Service originally estimated the work planned for all five sites would have required at least 10 years of consistent volunteer recruitment and direct management by the Forest Service to accomplish. Mark Rey, Under Secretary for Natural Resources and Environment, USDA, stated that –

ArrowCorps

ORDER OF THE ARROW • BOY SCOUTS OF AMERICA

Frankly, without the Order of the Arrow's leadership and dedicated service, the Forest Service would not have been able to perform the much needed work planned for each site. The projected wildlife and environmental benefits alone are significant. But, we also hoped that the Order of the Arrow's example of leadership in service would inspire other volunteer groups to provide additional needed service to our forest lands.

ArrowCorps[5] served to further the legacy of service established in the early days of the Scouting movement through programs such as the Eagle Scout Trail Building program of the 1920s and '30s. The programmatic details for the opening and closing gatherings at each site, and the servant leadership, team building, and sustainability training modules used during the work week with participants were developed by the OA's youth leadership. The on-site program was directed at training and encouraging youth and adult participants and staff to embrace the concepts learned and practiced during the week, return enthused to their local council, and successfully implement the concepts of service in their communities.

Now, Make It Happen at Home

During the planning and development of the project we hoped it would inspire participants to internalize the values of initiative, fellowship, teamwork, and servant leadership, to take home those lessons learned through hard work and example, and to eagerly apply those values and lessons at home in service to their council, community, and country. We are convinced that it did just that! As we approach the 100th anniversary of the Boy Scouts of America, we are encouraging local council leadership to identify a meaningful service project that could be planned and executed by council and lodge membership to benefit public property such as a municipal park, community center, state park, national forest, or national park.

Project Accomplishments

With the theme *"Five Sites, Five Weeks, Five Thousand Arrowmen"* – ArrowCorps[5] proved to be the largest service project conducted by the Boy Scouts of America since World War II. It is the largest single volunteer service project ever received by

the Forest Service in its rich 103 year history! Overall, through the efforts of 3,600 participants and staff, the OA provided 280,000 volunteer service hours worth $5.6 million to the Forest Service.

Throughout the summer the project was well received and strongly supported by the surrounding communities. Priceless media coverage was generated at each site, resulting in a total of 97 print articles, 34 television reports, and 95 online and radio reports on the volunteer service provided by the Boy Scouts of America through ArrowCorps[5]. *"All Work and No Play . . . ArrowCorps[5]'s Lasting Legacy in Wyoming's Tetons"* was featured on the cover of the May-June 2009 issue of *Scouting* magazine. Inside the magazine was a seven-page article entitled *"As Good as It Gets"*, summarizing the historical significance of ArrowCorps[5] to the BSA and U.S. Forest Service, and focusing specifically on the fun, fellowship, and accomplishments in the Bridger-Teton National Forest.

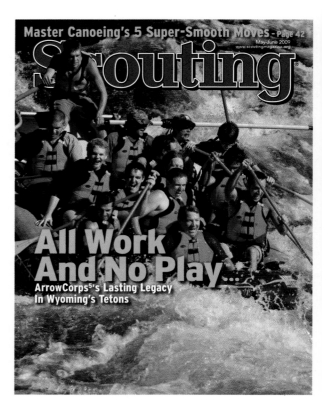

Site Specific Accomplishments
Mark Twain National Forest, Missouri – June 7 to 14, 2008

- 575 participants, staff, and U.S. Forest Service personnel
- Completed 134 acres and cut down more than 285,000 invasive Eastern Red Cedar trees
- Work exceeded original plans, resulting in restoration of a natural glade necessary for sustainability of the environment as well as wildlife in the area
- Base camp was constructed from scratch (no infrastructure available)
- U.S. Forest Service named area *"Arrowman's Glade"* at closing gathering

Manti-La Sal National Forest, Utah – June 14 to 21, 2008
- 463 participants, staff, U.S. Forest Service, and other agency personnel
- Completed approximately 13,000 acres or 33 miles of channel area affected by removing invasive Tamarisk, a non-native shrub harmful to other vegetation and wildlife
- 21 agencies involved, including Bureau of Land Management, Emery County, Emery County School District, and City of Huntington
- Work exceeded original project plans with less than half of the projected participants
- Patch auction raised $4,000; donated to the Canyon View Junior High School that served as base of operations

George Washington & Jefferson National Forests, Virginia – June 21 to 28, 2008
- 736 participants, staff, and U.S. Forest Service personnel
- Completed 8.3 miles of new multi-use trail (hiking/backpacking, mountain biking, and equestrian), repaired and improved miles of existing trail, constructed and installed four information kiosks and 86 trail signs, and surveyed and constructed seven camping platforms and adjoining trails made of treated lumber frames and compacted pea gravel
- Work far exceeded original plans
- Goshen Scout Reservation served as primary base camp
- During closing gathering, U.S. Forest Service named new multi-use trail along Peter's Ridge the "ArrowCorps Loop"

Shasta-Trinity National Forest, California – July 12 to 19, 2008
- 600 participants, staff, and U.S. Forest Service personnel (from all 50 states, Japan, and Taiwan)
- Removed 22 tons of illegally dumped trash, constructed or reconstructed more than 75 miles of trail on Pacific Crest Trail, Sisson-Callahan Trail, and McCloud Loop Trail, and rebuilt a lookout tower and four "comfort stations"
- National Chief Jake Wellman, Western Region Chief Mark Hendricks, and Youth Incident Commander Alex Braden were presented President's Volunteer Service Award by President George W. Bush during his visit to Redding, California
- Project exceeded all expectations and met all goals
- Mt. Shasta Ski Park served as primary base camp

Bridger-Teton National Forest, Wyoming – July 26 to August 2, 2008
- 1034 participants and staff, plus U.S. Forest Service personnel
- Completed more than 12 miles of multi-use trail on the Teton Pass, removed allotment fencing and 10 miles of exclusion fencing, constructed off-highway vehicle closures and wash bars, and provided campsite maintenance
- Project went above and beyond expectations; with early completion of planned projects, a fuels reduction project consisting of accumulation and piling of residual slash from cutting operations was developed and completed on 17 acres, and the group provided support to the U.S. Forest Service firefighting effort in the New Forks area north of Pinedale
- Patch auction raised $5,000; donated equally to Jackson Hole High School, which served as the base of operations for the project, and Friends of Pathways, a nonprofit organization that assisted with the project
- U.S. Forest Service named the new trail at Teton Pass the "Arrow Trail" during the Friday closing gathering

Reflection

Reconstructing this brief history of the *ArrowCorps*[5] project was a labor of love; it required rummaging through file drawers, boxes, email messages, and making a number of telephone calls to confirm recollection and facts. And, while I take full responsibility for any errors discovered in this narrative, it is but one person's perspective on a life-changing event. Each person who participated in *ArrowCorps*[5] contributed to its unparalleled success, creating their own story along the trail. That is the essence of the Scouting experience.

As I reflect back on last summer, I vividly recall the joy on the faces of each youth and adult I met as they lost themselves in the fellowship and service of others. It was a rare privilege and a blessing to have been involved with this project. I am deeply grateful for the opportunity to have worked alongside my devoted colleagues in the Order of the Arrow and the dedicated professionals of the U.S. Forest Service as we focused on one vision and partnered together to achieve one goal. To each person who made *ArrowCorps*[5] a reality please accept my heartfelt appreciation for your leadership in service. *ArrowCorps*[5] truly was *A Higher Adventure*.

Bradley E. Haddock, Chairman, National Order of the Arrow Committee
July 4, 2009

CHAPTER IV

MARK TWAIN
NATIONAL FOREST

JUNE 7 - 14, 2008

ArrowCorps[5] is the largest, most complex, most challenging conservation project ever conceived by the Order of Arrow and the Boy Scouts of America.

Jacob P. Wellman, 2008 National Chief, Order of the Arrow, BSA

When a kid talks about the ecosystem that we are involving and participating in, that's exciting.

Matt Walker, Incident Commander, Mark Twain National Forest

Mark Twain National Forest in Missouri was the setting for the opening of *ArrowCorps⁵*, the largest single service project in the history of the BSA, and the largest volunteer project undertaken by the U.S. Forest Service in its long history. Mark Twain was chosen as the site for the removal of invasive cedar trees from the forest's glades to restore native habitat. Some of the many different types of species in the Forest are in danger of becoming extinct, because of habitat destruction, overexploitation, or other environmental factors. Mark Twain has potential habitat for 14 federally Threatened, Endangered, and candidate species in Missouri. They are the gray bat, Indiana bat, bald eagle, Hine's emerald dragonfly, pink mucket pearly, Scaleshell, Spectalcase, Sheepnose, Tumbling Creek cavesnail, Topeka shiner, Ozark hellbender, Mead's milkweed, running buffalo clover, and Virginia sneezeweed. Restoring the habitat would perform a vital role in protecting these threatened species.

It is a land of surprisingly steep limestone mountains, clear rushing streams perfect for canoeing, and remarkably diverse plant life that supports the wide variety of species. Lying mostly in the Ozark Plateau, the Forest covers 1.5 million acres that was once given up for dead after timbering operations cleared these hills by the turn of the 20th Century. Careful stewardship has brought the forest back to life, now holding some of the Midwest's wildest, most remote land. The participants in *ArrowCorps⁵* worked in the Glade Top Trail area south of Ava, Missouri, removing invasive cedar trees from glade areas in the forest that would restore forest natural communities, and increase the sustainability of the environment, as well as the wildlife in the area.

The work done at Mark Twain kicked off an outstanding beginning to *ArrowCorps⁵* that was best exemplified by the enthusiastic slogan of the week: *"There are Arrowmen, then there are Mark Twain Arrowmen!"* Matthew M. Walker, Incident Commander, and Don Combs, Youth Incident Commander, provided the leadership that led the team to a resounding success. The *Instructor Corps*, led by David C. Dowty, further insured the success of the project by providing the invaluable backbone to the Mark Twain Project and all succeeding projects throughout the summer. Their experience, example and passion for the project were a significant factor in the success of the program and the excellent overall safety record for all five projects. The Incident Commanders at all five sites frequently credited the *Instructor Corps* for the success of *ArrowCorps⁵* stating that "we couldn't have pulled it off without them." Clyde Mayer, Director, National OA; Brad Haddock, Chairman, National OA Committee; and Jacob (Jake) P. Wellman, 2008 National Chief, OA; visited every site and contributed their leadership to each of the five sites over the summer of 2008, along with Tim Beaty, National Partnership Coordinator, US Forest Service.

With approximately 575 staff, participants, and U.S. Forest Service personnel involved, the project exceeded the original plans, and ultimately restored a natural glade. The team completed 134 acres and cut down more than 285,000 Eastern Red Cedar trees ranging in size from smaller than one inch in diameter to more than 18 inches in diameter.

One of the biggest challenges facing the team was the need to construct a base camp from "scratch" because there was no infrastructure available to support a camp serving as the base of operations. The team rose to the challenge despite the rainy weather; the lack of communications; and the loss of a fuel supplier who broke his contract the day before the participants arrived; and, managed to create a town for more than 600 people where nothing had existed before, all without causing a negative impact on the environment. The capable Communications Crew established complete radio, telephone, and internet communications in the middle of a remote valley; and the Material Supply Team found another source of fuel within 30 minutes of the arrival of participants. Everyone worked well together, including *ArrowCorps⁵* participants, staff, crew, local participants and National Forest Service personnel. 6 weeks after the week-long conservation work was completed, there was no evidence of the temporary town of 600 people, only the presence of a peaceful glade that once had been an Eastern Red Cedar tree forest.

Several representatives of the BSA visited the site including: James J. Terry, Assistant Chief Scout Executive and Chief Financial Officer; Frank Riegelman, Director, Camping and Conservation; and Brad Farmer, Central Region Director. Each was very impressed with what he saw. Jim Terry exclaimed to Brad Haddock that the team had *"knocked it out of the park."* After the pouring rain stopped, the Friday night gathering was a wonderful time of celebration. Paul Strong, Acting Supervisor, Mark Twain National Forest, U.S. Forest Service (and fellow Eagle Scout and Arrowman), congratulated the staff and participants on an outstanding project. The Forest Service personnel could not have been happier and announced that the glade was named the *Arrowman Glade* and unveiled a facsimile of the signage at the closing gathering. Mark Rey, Under Secretary for Natural Resources

and Environment, US Department of Agriculture, was unable to visit the site on Friday, because of the weather, but sent his best wishes and attended the Manti-La Sal National Forest site the following week. Terri S. Haddock, wife of Brad Haddock, and Mason Thomas, Southern Region Chief, BSA; also visited the site and boosted the morale, as did the special appearances by Smokey Bear and Woodsy Owl who cheered on the Arrowmen's conservation work at the first of five sites in five national forests.

Several other groups provided their capable assistance at the Mark Twain site including: Mingo Job Corps; Taney County Emergency Medical Service; David Norman, Ava Drug Company; St. John's Emergency Trauma Center; DJ Satterfield, Life Line Air Medical Support; John Miller, Naturalist Program Supervisor of the Shepherd of the Hills Conservation Center; and the Bradleyville Volunteer Fire Department. Each played a special role in the success of the project.

Multiple lessons were learned or reinforced: the value of investing in the time to train all participants for safety; the benefit of daily entertainment; the power of everyone working together to keep up morale; and the value of recognizing the resourceful talents of the local participants whose help made significant contributions to the success of the project. Each person who participated in the Mark Twain project can be proud that he or she helped to ensure the long-term sustainability of a glade in this biologically rich ecological resource, now known to all as *Arrowman Glade*.

At the end of the week, the *Instructor Corps* received a standing ovation from the participants for their outstanding work before they left on Friday morning for Manti-La Sal National Forest. Everyone was excited about the project, enjoying the opportunity to serve, and prepared to attend the next *ArrowCorps⁵* event.

AC5 | MARK TWAIN NATIONAL FOREST

AC5 | MARK TWAIN NATIONAL FOREST

AC5 | MARK TWAIN NATIONAL FOREST

AC5 | MARK TWAIN NATIONAL FOREST

CHAPTER V

MANTI-LA SAL NATIONAL FOREST

JUNE 14 - 21, 2008

This project provided a once-in-a-lifetime opportunity for each participant to set an example of leadership in service to those who treasure our national forests.

Bradley E. Haddock, Chairman, National Order of the Arrow Committee, BSA

This is a project where we can actually do something that impacts not only the water resources but the habitat for the vegetation and the critters.

Jack Hess, Incident Commander, Manti-La Sal National Forest

Manti-La Sal National Forest, located in southeastern Utah, was chosen as one of the five sites for *ArrowCorps⁵* to remove tamarisk, an invasive species, to protect the mountainous desert landscapes and remaining records of ancient peoples who came before us, like the Paleo-Indians, Desert Archaic, Fremont, and Anasazi. Tamarisk limits the amount of water available for the establishment of native vegetation. The lack of native vegetation limits the wildlife habitat and does not allow the watershed to function properly.

The Manti Division of the national forest has high elevation lakes, diverse vegetation, nearly vertical escarpments and areas of scenic and geologic interest. The La Sal Division-Moab has mountain peaks up to 12,000 feet in elevation, and canyons and forests, in sharp contrast to the hot red-rock landscape of Arches and Canyonlands National Parks. The *ArrowCorps⁵* conservation service project's goal was to remove tamarisk to enhance wildlife habitat and restore a healthy environment and protect the cultural and historical significance of the area.

John ("Jack") W. Hess, Incident Commander, and John Fagan, Youth Incident Commander, led the Incident Command team on a very successful *ArrowCorps⁵* project to remove invasive plants at Manti-La Sal, reflected in the week's group yell: "*Death to Tamarisk.*" Approximately 13,000 acres or 33 miles of channel area around Joe's Valley Reservoir and Dry Walsh on the Manti-La Sal and in the Buckhorn Wash on Bureau of Land Management land were affected by the removal of tamarisk, the non-native shrub harmful to other vegetation and wildlife. As with the Mark Twain results, this was more than the original planned project with less than half the projected number of participants. There were a total of 463 participants and staff, made up of 145 participants, 165 staff, 43 *Instructor Corps* members and 110 agency personnel. Twenty-one different agencies were involved in the project, including the U.S. Forest Service, the Bureau of Land Management, Emery County, Emery County School District, and the City of Huntington.

Tom Fitzgibbon, Director, Western Region, BSA; Mike Neider, member, National Boy Scout Committee and Second Counselor of the Young Men Presidency of the Latter Day Saints Church, visited the site during the week. Utah Lieutenant Governor Gary R. Herbert visited on Wednesday evening and really connected with the group with his comments. Pamela E. Brown, Supervisor, Manti-La Sal Forest, visited the conservation work sites, too, along with Hilary Gordon, Mayor, City of Huntington, Utah; the Huntington City Council members: Cathy Cowley, Norman Dingman, Julie A. Jones and Bob T. Mills; and the Emery County Commissioners: Gary Kofford, Chairman; Laurie Pitchforth and Jeff Horrocks. Benjamin Stilwill, 2008 National Vice Chief; and John Fagan made a presentation to the Huntington City Council on Wednesday evening. Mark Rey visited the site on Friday evening and spoke to the group during the closing gathering. Bill Steele, Director, National Eagle Scout Association, and member of the Boy Scout Division staff, visited the site on Thursday and toured the various work areas with Jack Hess and Brad Haddock. Smokey

Bear and Woodsy Owl again cheered on the Arrowmen's conservation work. The successful completion of more goals than originally planned with fewer participants demonstrated everyone's enthusiasm for the project.

Other groups that assisted were Emery County Weed & Pest; Carbon County Weed & Pest; Skyline Coordinated Weed Management Area; Utah State University Extension Service; Castleland Rural Conservation & Development Council; Emery County Water Conservancy District; Utah Backcountry Volunteers; San Rafael Conservation District; Canyon View Junior High School; Emery County School District; City of Huntington; Utah Department of Natural Resources; Utah State Institutional Trust Lands; Utah Department of Agriculture; Utah Department of Forestry, Fire, & State Lands; Utah Division of Water Quality; Utah Division of Wildlife Resources; National Park Service; Emery County Sheriffs Office; Rocky Mountain Power; Dow Chemical; Bureau of Reclamation; and National Fish and Wildlife Foundation - Pulling Together Initiative. Each group contributed significantly to the success of Manti-La Sal.

At the conclusion of the work week, a patch auction was held that raised more than $4,000. This money was donated to the Canyon View Junior High School which served as the base of operations. The project also received considerable media attention, including an article in the *Salt Lake Tribune*. The City Council served ice cream and cookies to the entire group Friday evening after the closing gathering.

The biggest lesson from the event is to never underestimate the power of a committed group of people. As Margaret Mead said, "*Never doubt that a small group of thoughtful, committed citizens can change the world; indeed; it's the only thing that ever has.*"

AC5 | MANTI-LA SAL NATIONAL FOREST

AC5 | MANTI-LA SAL NATIONAL FOREST

AC5-J. MANTI-LA SAL NATIONAL FOREST

AC5 | MANTI-LA SAL NATIONAL FOREST

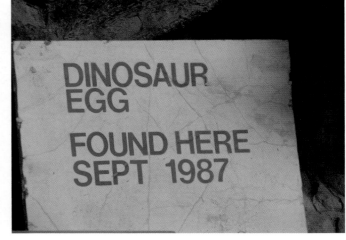

DINOSAUR
EGG

FOUND HERE
SEPT 1987

AC5 | MANTI-LA SAL NATIONAL FOREST

CHAPTER VI

GEORGE WASHINGTON & JEFFERSON NATIONAL FORESTS

JUNE 21 - 28, 2008

It's natural for the Boy Scouts to work with the Forest Service.

Clyde Mayer, Director, National Order of the Arrow, BSA

All of the Arrowmen know what they have done and the lasting impact that they will have on the environment. I agree with one of the Forest Service engineers that said "If this is what's going to lead our country in the future, then we're okay."

Ron Bell, Incident Commander, George Washington-Jefferson National Forests

The combined George Washington and Jefferson National Forests were chosen as the location for one of the five sites for *ArrowCorps⁵* because work was needed to repair and improve trails within the 1.8 million acre recreational area that includes part of the Appalachian National Scenic Trail and 15 designated wildernesses, among other spectacular features. The *ArrowCorps⁵* conservation service project would help the land to recover from the effects of historic land use practices and major storms, keeping Forest visitors on the trails and out of the habitat of threatened species.

The Forests are located in the beautiful Blue Ridge Mountains of Virginia, home to a wide variety of species, including at least 70 amphibians and reptiles, neo-tropical birds, and approximately 200 species of birds. There are at least 55 species of mammals ranging from white-tailed deer to black bears and ruffed grouse, to several very rare species, including the water shrew and rock vole. There are more than 100 species of freshwater fishes and mussels, with 26 of these listed as Threatened, Endangered, or Sensitive. Twenty-seven of the plants and animal species found in the Forests are listed as Threatened of Endangered. Everyone eagerly undertook the task of restoring these beautiful lands to protect the habitat of the many endangered species.

The fine weather allowed L. Ronald Bell, Incident Commander, and Geoff Landau, a Section Chief and Youth Incident Commander, to lead the team of 685 participants and staff at George Washington & Jefferson to provide more than 71,000 hours of service and complete the priority list of projects. The team rallied their forces during the week with the affectionate reference to their project as "*GW and Jeff.*" Although there were the predictable, minor medical issues that accompany a group this large working in the woods, there were no injuries. Participants and staff had the option of white-water rafting the New River in West Virginia or touring the historical sites in the Lexington, Virginia area. Water skiing, fly fishing, mountain biking and hiking were also available in camp.

Jim Terry made his second *ArrowCorps⁵* visit on Thursday. Other visitors included Patrick Rooney, Northeast Region Chief and, Al Lambert, Scout Executive, National Capital Area Council. Jim Terry visited various sites to see the outstanding work on the camp platforms and trails at Camp Moomaw along with trails in the James River area. Everyone appreciated the special visits from Smokey Bear and Woodsy Owl who came to recognize the OAs great work in the national forests.

Lake Merriweather and the beautiful mountains provided the backdrop for the closing gathering on Friday night at Goshen. Jim Terry told the gathering that when he and the others first heard about the *ArrowCorps⁵* project they thought it was a "*hair brained idea*," but that they knew if anyone could pull off the project it was the Order of the Arrow. He noted that the participants and staff had "*moved way beyond irksome tasks*" and were living out cheerful service. Gloria Manning, Associate Deputy Chief National Forest System, U.S. Forest Service, arrived from Washington, D.C. to visit the site on Friday. She was quite impressed with the work completed and had the opportunity during the gathering to emotionally express her congratulations and thanks to the participants and staff. Maureen Hyzer, Forest Supervisor, George Washington and Jefferson National Forests, announced the new multi-use trail would be known as *ArrowCorps Loop* and, to a rousing round of applause, presented one of the new trail signs to Geoff Landau.

Working with 51 U.S. Forest Service employees, 8.2 miles of new multi-use trail (hiking, backpacking, mountain biking and equestrian) were completed along Peter's Ridge; miles of existing trail were repaired and improved; four information kiosks were constructed and installed; six camping platforms were surveyed and constructed along with surveying and constructing adjoining trails out of compacted pea gravel. Five articles on the George Washington and Jefferson National Forests project appeared on the front page of various local newspapers while we were there. There were several TV and radio reports and interviews during the week. Participants continued to ask when this would be done again. Many commented that this

event was the best OA or Scouting event in which they had ever participated. The *Instructor Corps* continued to do a great job.

After George Washington and Jefferson National Forest, the *Instructor Corps* spent a short time at Philmont for a little rest during the week. The excitement continued to grow with the successful completion of another of the five sites, along with the awareness that the OA was continuing and expanding its exemplary history of servant leadership. Each participant and staff member knew their hard work, leadership, and dedication were part of the growing legacy of the Brotherhood of the OA and cherished the honor.

AC5 | GEORGE WASHINGTON & JEFFERSON NATIONAL FORESTS

AC5 | GEORGE WASHINGTON & JEFFERSON NATIONAL FORESTS

CHAPTER VII

SHASTA-TRINITY
NATIONAL FOREST

JULY 12 - 19, 2008

ArrowCorps[5] was a success on so many fronts. How many volunteer organizations come to the U.S. Forest Service wanting to do service? That's a phenomenal success just in itself. The Order of the Arrow exceeded the U.S. Forest Service expectations at every site.

Tim Beaty, National Partnership Coordinator, U.S. Forest Service

The Instructor Corps was terrific . . . they've done a wonderful job. The United States Forest Service here — there is nothing I could do to thank them enough!

Steven D. Bradley, Incident Commander, Shasta-Trinity National Forest

The largest forest in California, Shasta-Trinity National Forest, covers 2.1 million acres of diverse landscape located in the beautiful Cascade Mountains of northern California, at the foot of Mt. Shasta. It was chosen as one of the five sites for *ArrowCorps[5]* because it needed trash removal to help maintain clean water and a healthy forest, and trail work to enhance access to its scenic areas.

The land in Shasta-Trinity ranges from 1,000 feet to 14,162 feet in elevation, and encompasses five wilderness areas, hundreds of mountain lakes, and 6,278 miles of streams and rivers, including a large manmade lake in the Whiskeytown-Shasta-Trinity National Recreation Area where there are active bald eagle nest territories. The entire National Recreation Area serves as intermediate winter range for Columbia black-tailed deer with critical winter range on most of the south-facing slopes, especially on the east side of the reservoirs. There are more than 60 pairs of osprey, and large deer and bear populations. Most of the area is covered in Mixed Conifers that have been impacted by changes made in human activity in the last century, evidenced by the frequent fires, eroding soil, and excessive sediment in the water of the area. The *ArrowCorps[5]* conservation service project would help to reverse some of these negative impacts to restore the natural habitat that sustains the wildlife.

Fortunately, the terrible forest fires that raged during the week of the conservation work only came within 30 miles of the work location and had little effect on the project. The weather cooperated even though the haze was visible toward the south. All of the goals were met and exceeded under the capable direction of Steven D. Bradley, Incident Commander, and his team, including Alex Braden, Youth Incident Commander, who initially recruited Arrowmen volunteers with "*Hasta Be Shasta*" and then personified their individual commitment to the project during the week of work with the motto "*Leave your EGO at the Door, Be Rigidly, Flexible.*"

With 600 participants, staff, and agency personnel (from all 50 states, Japan and Taiwan) at the Shasta-Trinity project, more than 22 tons of illegally dumped garbage was removed from the forest. In addition, the construction, maintenance, or reconstruction of more than 100 miles of trail on the Pacific Crest Trail, the Sisson-Callahan Trail, and the McCloud Loop Trail was completed. A lookout tower and four euphemistically named "comfort stations" along the trails were rebuilt, too. By the end of the project, the work on the Shasta-Trinity conservation service project exceeded expectations. Importantly, all of the work was done safely with no injuries, just some minor cuts and scratches.

On Friday, participants and staff had the option of playing golf at the Mt. Shasta Resort, visiting Lassen National Park, touring the caverns, or participating at the beach party and catered lunch at Siskiyou Lake. A few of the really "hard core" members of the *Instructor Corps* hiked to the 14,162 foot summit of Mt. Shasta.

Several representatives of the BSA National office visited the Shasta site, including Al Kugler, Director, Office of the Chief Scout Executive; George Trosko, Director, Boy Scout Division; John Van Dreese, Associate Region Director, Program, Western Region; and Tom Fitzgibbon; each venturing into the backcountry to greet the crews and see the great work being done. Mark Hendricks, Western Region Chief, also visited the site, rallying the crew. Joel Holtrop, Deputy

Chief, U.S. Forest Service, toured the work sites with several officials from the Shasta-Trinity National Forest included: John Heibel, Forest Engineer; Ken Kellogg, Assistant Forest Engineer; Steve Naser, Trails and Facilities Engineer; Sharon Heywood, Forest Supervisor; and Kathleen Jordan, Program Management Officer. Special appreciation is extended to Sharon Heywood and Kathleen Jordan for their contributions. Kathleen worked tirelessly for more than three years on this project. She is a Brotherhood Member and was instrumental in arranging the visit by President George W. Bush and in raising significant community support for the project.

Other groups that assisted the Shasta-Trinity project included: Sam Burrows and the Back Country Horsemen; Shasta College; Shasta County Board of Supervisors; and local community leaders who wish to remain anonymous. Mt. Shasta Ski Park served as the base camp and project headquarters. The team appreciated the opportunity to work with the owners, Andy Garcia and Chuck Young, who graciously opened the ski lift and hosted a reception Thursday evening for the Incident Command staff and guests at the top of the lift. Andy is an Eagle Scout, Chuck is a Life Scout, and Chuck's son, Jason, is an Eagle Scout. Thursday was a mountain top experience for everyone. Andy, Chuck and Jason wanted to know when we would be back.

The stars were out and the sky clear on Friday evening during the closing gathering. Sharon Heywood participated in the opening gathering and returned to thank the group for a job well done. Joel Holtrop explained that the *ArrowCorps[5]* project not only represented the largest single service project ever undertaken by the Boy Scouts of America, it also represented the largest volunteer project ever received by the U.S. Forest Service. Mark Rey made his second visit and thanked the group for their outstanding accomplishments. He is an Eagle Scout, Vigil Honor member, and father of an Eagle Scout. Mark worked with us from the early days of this project and his support, guidance, and personal participation in the *ArrowCorps[5]* project are sincerely appreciated.

AC5 | SHASTA-TRINITY NATIONAL FOREST

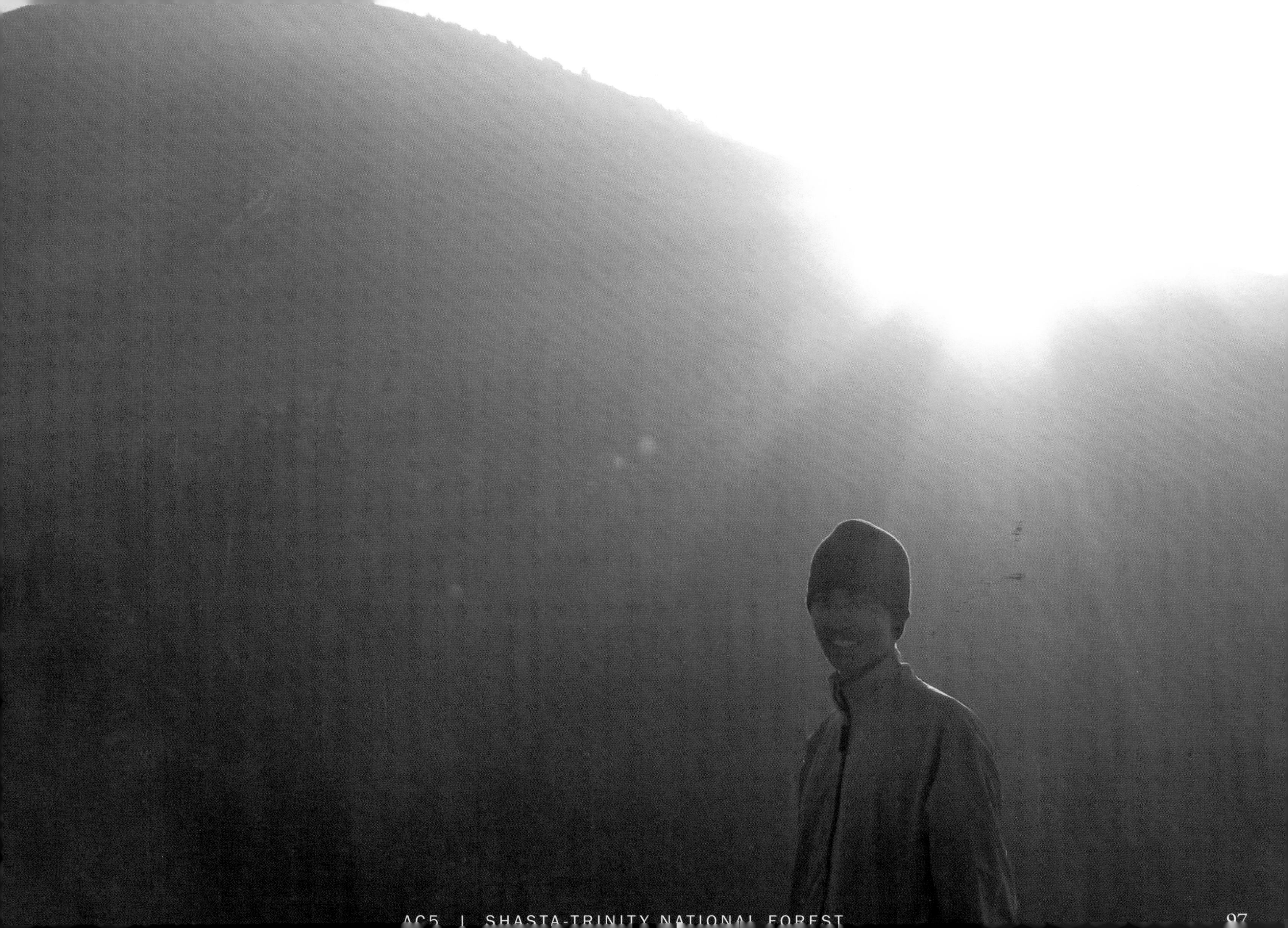

AC5 | SHASTA-TRINITY NATIONAL FOREST

AC5 | SHASTA-TRINITY NATIONAL FOREST

AC5 | SHASTA-TRINITY NATIONAL FOREST

AC5 | SHASTA-TRINITY NATIONAL FOREST

AC5 | SHASTA-TRINITY NATIONAL FOREST

CHAPTER VIII

BRIDGER-TETON NATIONAL FOREST

JULY 26 - AUGUST 2, 2008

Your work on the five National Forest sites is the kind of thing that you will bring your grandchildren back to see. You have made a difference on the land and the American people thank you for that.

Abigail Kimbell, Forest Service Chief, U.S. Forest Service

One of the Forest Service members told us earlier this week if we were working on Teton Pass through our normal process of bringing in volunteers it would take us 10 years to do what the Order of the Arrow did this week.

This project has surpassed all of our expectations – it's made a difference. The Forest Service recognizes it, the community recognizes it. So, in another three weeks when we are all back home, I think we are going to look back and say, this ArrowCorps[5] – this Bridger-Teton project – changed a community and changed how the community looks at Scouting and the Order of the Arrow.

Daniel T. Segersin, Incident Commander, Bridger-Teton National Forest

Bridger-Teton National Forest was selected as a site for *ArrowCorps⁵* for three reasons. First, deadwood needed to be removed, because it creates a serious fire threat to the life of the forest. Second, the forest was constricted by the presence of miles of fencing that restricted the movement of wildlife. Removing the fencing would create an open range for large wildlife, such as elk, moose, antelope, mule deer, bear and wolf, that would improve feeding when food is scarce; improve breeding, birthing and grazing; reduce the transmission of diseases; remove the risk of injury or death to the animals that try to jump over the fence; and restore wildlife migration patterns. Third, high-elevation, multi-use trails needed to be repaired and rebuilt.

Bridger-Teton is located in western Wyoming and is the second largest National Forest outside of Alaska. It consists of 3.4 million acres reaching from Grand Teton National Park, located just south of Yellowstone National Park, along the boundaries of the Shoshone National Forest and the Washakie Wilderness down to south central Lincoln County. Located within the forest are the Gros Ventre, Bridger, and Teton Wildernesses, totaling 1.2 million acres. The tallest mountain in Wyoming is found in the forest, Gannett Peak, at 13,804 feet, along with the Gros Ventre landslide, which is one of the largest readily visible landslides on earth. The Forest makes up a large part of the 20 million acre Greater Yellowstone Ecosystem, the largest intact ecosystem in the lower 48 United States.

ArrowCorps⁵ volunteered to address the serious fire issues; to help remove the fence restricting movement of wildlife; and to construct new trails to separate mountain bike riders and horseback riders. *ArrowCorps⁵* proposed to: complete the *Arrow Trail* at Teton Pass, a five mile stretch of the single-track mountain bike trail, and three other trails that make up an 11 mile trail system that linked pre-existing trails. In addition, the plan was to remove 8,000 feet of the 10 foot high, sheep wire fence with barbed wire on top, known as the Goosewing Exclusion Fence near the Gros Ventre River and wilderness area; and also to remove three miles of barbed wire fence and posts near the Gros Ventre River.

Headquarters were set up at Jackson Hole High School near the National Forest office, where staff, equipment, and supplies were coordinated for the work during the week. The team proudly cheered their slogan to inspire the Bridger-Teton crew: *"Totally" - - Tetons!"* Remarkably, the team, staff, and participants were able to accomplish much more than initially planned, thanks to the capable leadership of Daniel T. Segersin, Incident Commander, and his team, including Sam Fife, Youth Incident Commander, with their call to service. The setting was gorgeous and the weather was perfect, ranging from the mid 80s during the day to the low 40s overnight. With 1,034 participants and staff, plus Forest Service personnel from Bridger-Teton National Forest, the group completed more than 12 miles of multi-use trail on the Teton Pass; removed 10 miles of the exclusion fence and completed additional small projects in the Goosewing area; and, removed allotment fences, constructed off-highway vehicle closures, constructed wash bars, provided general campsite maintenance at Soda Lake campground, and other additional projects in the Gros Ventre area. In recognition of the OAs work, the new trail at Teton Pass was named the *Arrow Trail*.

Representatives from the National BSA who visited along with Brad Haddock, Clyde Mayer, and Jake Wellman at the site included Robert J. Mazzuca, Chief Scout Executive; Al Kugler; George Trosko; John Green, Director, Program; Perry Cochell, National Senior Endowment Counsel; Wayne Perry, International Commissioner; and Tom Fitzgibbon. They visited the site and went into the backcountry to greet the crews and see the great work being done. In addition, other representatives of the local

Scouts visited the site to lend their support, including: Howard Bulloch, Council President, Las Vegas Area Council; Phil Bevins, Scout Executive, Las Vegas Area Council; and Clarke Farrer, Scout Executive, Grand Teton Council; along with the indefatigable Smokey Bear and Woodsy Owl who continued to cheer on the Arrowmen's conservation work through the last of the five sites.

Grace Ohlhaut, Associate Director, USA Freedom Corps, Office of the White House, and Governor David D. Freudenthal and his wife, Nancy, Governor of Wyoming, toured the work sites, along with Mark Rey; Abigail Kimbell, Chief, U.S. Forest Service; Gloria Manning; and Niffy Hamilton, Forest Supervisor, Bridger-Teton National Forest. Because of the successful early completion of several planned projects, a fuels reduction project consisting of the accumulation and piling of residual slash from cutting operations was developed and completed on 15 acres in the Fall Creek area and on more than two acres in the Granite Creek area (which included a Girl Scout camp). The group also provided support to the Forest Service firefighting effort in the New Forks fire north of Pinedale. All of the work was performed safely, with no injuries other than minor cuts and scratches and some altitude sickness. Recreation was provided throughout the week, allowing each participant and staff member to take a day to enjoy either whitewater rafting, a float trip, a tour of Yellowstone National Park, or just hanging around Jackson.

The team overcame the challenge of communications, both within Teton Pass and with the two remote locations, where radios did not have sufficient range and the range of the U.S. Forest Service radios was limited; and where the cellular telephone service in the pass was intermittent. The team sent a Forest Service employee and an *ArrowCorps⁵* staffer up the mountain each day to operate a repeater station to resolve the problem enabling the crews on the mountain to communicate with the repeater station, who would then relay a message to the High School base operation or vice-versa. Additionally, there was a volunteer Communications Officer who was a licensed HAM Radio Operator, who used his personal transceiver and antenna setup to monitor radio traffic.

Other groups that helped in the success of *ArrowCorps⁵* at Bridger-Teton included: Bridger-Teton U.S. Forest Service Staff; Rotary Club of Jackson; Teton Whitewater; Grand Teton Council, BSA; Jackson Wildlife Foundation; and John Deere, Bonneville County Implement, Idaho Falls, Idaho.

In addition to exemplary work performed in the Bridger-Teton National Forest, an auction of Order of the Arrow patches was held that raised $5,000. This sum was donated equally to Jackson Hole High School, which served as the base of operations for the project, and to Friends of Pathway, a non-profit organization that helped with the project.

Valuable lessons were learned by the *ArrowCorps⁵* crew working with the U.S. Forest Service at Bridger Teton National Forest that can be applied to other large service projects that involve a large number of participants and several agencies or groups working together, such as the need to make careful plans; a back-up plan; and then to practice all of the plans. In other words, be prepared, make safety a priority, and practice Leave No Trace principles.

AC5 | BRIDGER-TETON NATIONAL FOREST

AC5 BRIDGER TETON NATIONAL FOREST

AC5 | BRIDGER-TETON NATIONAL FOREST

PRESIDENT BUSH PRESENTS PRESIDENT'S VOLUNTEER SERVICE AWARD

I want to thank the Boy Scouts of America for their work in the forest with the U.S. Forest Service. You are the leaders of the future.

President George W. Bush during the presentation of the President's Volunteer Service Award to the Order of the Arrow, BSA

President George W. Bush recognized the extraordinary contributions made by the Order of the Arrow to the National Forest Service with the historic undertaking of *ArrowCorps*[5]. During a Presidential visit to Redding, California, on July 17, 2008, President George W. Bush awarded the prestigious President's Volunteer Service Award to Jacob P. Wellman, 2008 National Chief; Mark Hendricks, Western Region Chief; and, Alex Braden, Youth Incident Commander, *ArrowCorps*[5] Shasta-Trinity, in recognition of their instrumental roles in the long-range planning and execution of *ArrowCorps*[5], the largest national service project since World War II.

Jake Wellman, Mark Hendricks, and Alex Braden joined Governor Arnold Schwarzenegger, California; and Mayor Mary Leas Stegall, Redding, California; in front of Air Force One to welcome the President to the nearby Redding Municipal Airport where he arrived to begin a tour of the damage from the forest fires in the area. The President first greeted the Governor, the Mayor, and then the three Presidential Volunteer Service Award recipients, shaking their hands and presenting each one with a lapel pin to thank them for making a difference in the lives of others. Jake Wellman said that the President *"thanked us for being Scouts and thanked us for our hard work."* Alex Braden said that it was *"an immense honor to meet the President and represent the Order of the Arrow for the work the Order is doing in the National Forests this summer at ArrowCorps[5]."* Alex added that *"this award is for the thousands of Arrowmen across the country that have assisted in the planning and execution of this project."*

Later, the three award recipients served as part of the background contingent for the President when he made a press statement. They shook hands with the President again before his departure from Redding and then turned to the many press affiliates who interviewed, photographed and recorded the three new "national celebrities" for local evening news segments across the country. These Arrowmen exemplified servant leadership and represented all Arrowmen when they accepted the President's Volunteer Service Award. Each Arrowman who participated in *ArrowCorps*[5] demonstrated cheerful service, steadfast commitment, and selfless service, worthy of a Presidential Award. As Sharon Heywood stated: *"This recognition crystallizes the Scout habit of helpfulness into a life purpose of leadership in cheerful service to others."*

The Order of the Arrow is an official certifying organization for the President's Volunteer Service Award. In his January 2002 State of the Union Address, President Bush called on all Americans to make a difference in their communities through volunteer service. He created the USA Freedom Corps, Office of the White House, to strengthen and expand volunteer service by adults and youth, highlighting youth volunteer service. Americans are responding to the President's Call to Service. According to the Bureau of Labor Statistics, more than 61 million Americans volunteered in 2006.

The President's Volunteer Service Award was created at the President's direction by the President's Council on Service and Civic Participation. The Award is available to youth ages 14 and under who have completed 50 or more hours of volunteer service; to individuals 15 and older who have completed 100 or more hours; and to families or groups who have completed 200 or more hours. To date, more than 662,000 individuals have received the President's Volunteer Service Award. Arrowmen are encouraged to visit the President's Volunteer Service Award Web site for more information to receive the Presidential award for their volunteer service in connection with their work on the *ArrowCorps*[5] project or their volunteer service in their own home communities. To register for or obtain additional information on the award, please visit www.presidentialserviceawards.gov.

AC5 | PRESIDENTIAL VISIT

AC5 | PRESIDENTIAL VISIT

AC5 | PRESIDENTIAL VISIT

CHAPTER X

ArrowCorps⁵
PARTICIPANTS & STAFF

The coveted ArrowCorps⁵ arrowhead patch was presented during the Friday night closing gathering to every participant and staff member who successfully completed the week of service at each project site.

*ArrowCorps*5
A HIGHER ADVENTURE

 Mark Twain National Forest
Project Staff
June 7-June 14, 2008

ORDER OF THE ARROW   BOY SCOUTS OF AMERICA

*ArrowCorps*5
A HIGHER ADVENTURE

 Manti-La Sal National Forest
Project Staff
June 14-June 21, 2008

ORDER OF THE ARROW   BOY SCOUTS OF AMERICA

*ArrowCorps*5
A HIGHER ADVENTURE

 George Washington & Jefferson National Forests
Project Staff
June 21-June 28, 2008

ORDER OF THE ARROW   BOY SCOUTS OF AMERICA

*ArrowCorps*5
A HIGHER ADVENTURE

 Shasta-Trinity National Forest
Project Staff
July 12-July 19, 2008

ORDER OF THE ARROW   BOY SCOUTS OF AMERICA

*ArrowCorps*5
A HIGHER ADVENTURE

 Bridger-Teton National Forest
Project Staff
July 26-August 2, 2008

ORDER OF THE ARROW   BOY SCOUTS OF AMERICA

Mark Twain Staff

Amelse, Dick
Ast, David
Austin, George
Babb, Timothy
Bajan, Greg
Barnum, Chris
Barnum, Robert
Becker, Kyle
Beckman, Robert
Berger, Marcus
Bernal, Ken
Bloom, Dale
Bolles, Forrest
Bolles, Olivia
Bolton, Chris
Bolton, Eric
Bradbury, Nathan
Braddy, Ryan
Bresnahan, Russ
Brooking, Kevin
Brown, Earl Keith
Brown, Timothy
Bubeck, Brandon (William)
Bubeck, Harry
Bubeck, Nathan
Burns, Randall
Busse, Dan
Byrne, Sean
Caithaml, Michael
Carpenter, Greg
Carson, David
Caspari, Matt
Caves, Carl 'Randy'
Chapman, Jim
Chrzanowski, Brian
Clasing, Michael

Clossin, George
Combs, Don
Combs, Philip
Coning, Chris
Coning, Mitch
Coon, Jeff
Cope, Thom
Couch, Tyler
Courtney, Christopher
Cronen, Paul
Crume, Robert
Cummins, Timothy
Daniel, Mark
Davis, Jeffery
Dickson, Jimmy
Dillon, William
Doerflein, Greg
Donahue, John
Donahue, Michael
Donahue, Timothy
Dotson, Donald
Douty, David
Dunbar, Don
Dworak, Joe
Dye, Allen
Dysart, Simeon 'Sim'
Easterling, Ryan
Edwards, J.D.
Ellison, Roger
Emery, Ralph
Epstein, Brad
Even, Matthew
Eyman, Dick
Falcon, Noel
Ferolo, Richard
Ferrcino, Tony
Field, James

Fields, Mark
Flater, Michael
Flater, Scott
Flatt, Md, James
Fodero, Frank
Frankel, Neal
Franz, Eric
Frazee, Timothy
Frazier, Dan
Friedrichsen, Aaron
Furlow, Rasheed
Gaston, Grady
Gee, Michelle
Gildon, Fran
Gildon, Mark
Giles, Daniel
Gray, John
Grogan, Terry
Grove, Christopher
Hale, April
Hallmark, Carter
Hampton, Sue
Harbin, Charlie
Hargis, Darin
Harper, Kevin
Harris, Donald
Harris, Monte
Hawley, Don
Hayes, Jami
Haynes, Glenn
Henderson, Larry
Hipps, Joshua
Holland, Burl
Hooten, Jeff
Hruska, Thomas
Hudspeth, Eric
Huerter, Nathan

Hunt, Josh
Hylton, Scott
Isaacson, Paul
Ishmael, Banks
Ishmael, Bj
Jackowiak, Cameron
Jensen, Paul
Jilka, Brian
Johnson, Jo Ellen
Johnson, Judy
Johnson, Lewis David
Johnson, Patricia
Joyce, Thomas
Justice, Jay (Jeff)
Kammerer, Leland
Kappel, Steven
Kennedy, John
Keyser, Kevin
Kirlin, Josh
Kitterlin, Loren
Kitterlin, Patrick
Knudsen, Jake
Kriechbaum, Monika
Kriechbaum, Victor
Krochmal, Chuck
Larsen, James
Laturno, Michael
Leeser, Sally
Levitt, Bruce
Lichota, Brad
Lloyd, David
Lohsee, Alexander
Lombardo, Jach
Long, David
Long, Dean
Lucerne, Sherry
Ludwig, Benjamin

Mackey, Rodney
Marchant-Shapiro, Jesse
Marlatt, Christopher
Martens, Madeline
Martens, Rod
Mason, Robert
Mayer, Clyde
Mcdaniel, Isaac
Meaders, Kenneth
Meador, Ryan
Meier, Blake
Miller, Daniel
Miller, Steve
Miller, Terrel
Molt, Judy Lynn
Moore, Rich
Morrow, Jeffery
Morrow Ii, Jeffery
Moss, Robert
Munoz, Trinidad
Murphree, David
Nash, Robert
Nathan, Keith
Nathan, Marki
Neihoff, Zachery
Norris, Mark
Ollar, Alexis
O'Neill, Jack
Ongley, Craig
O'Shea, Timothy
Otis, Lori
Paquette, Jay
Parker, Alyx
Parrish, Gregory
Perra, Daniel
Petty, Richard

Phillips, Harold
Polk, Carroll
Price, Michael
Pulley, Sam
Radtke Iii, Robert
Raine, Phillip
Richardson, Jacob
Riedl, Tim
Riefle, Charles
Risse, John
Robin, Scott
Robson, Sheri
Robson, Willy
Rochowiak, Michael
Roehrig, Ronald
Ruggles, James
Salvini, Joseph
Schaeffer, Brian
Schaub, Dave
Scheffier, Scott
Scheffler, Darlene
Schildknecht, Chris
Schildknecht, William
Schreffler, Chris
Schudra, Josh
Scott, Harold
Scott, Steve
Semple, Glen
Shepperson, Sam
Sheren, Kirk
Sirhal, Bob
Skelly, Matt
Smalley, Colin
Sorensen, Robert
Southwick, Jacob
Spencer, Douglas
Spencer, Ryan

Starr, Te
Starr Jr, Thomas
Sturges, Frank
Sullivan, Bob
Sullivan, Michael
Swanson, Cody
Swedenburg, Keith
Swedenburg, Patsy
Taylor, Steve
Tennill, Jr, Clinton
Thomas, Ian
Thomas, Mason
Thompson, Scott
Tighe, Sean
Trust, Daniel
Trust, Edward
Trusty, Robert
Tschetter, Marty
Tyllick, Paul
Wagner, Robert
Walker, Matt
Wallace, Hugh
Weckhorst, David
Wedding, Daniel
Weiland, David
Wellman, Jake
Welpe, Dennis
Wernecke, Joseph
Wilbur, Mark
Williams, Gary
Williams, Virginia Eileen

Mark Twain Participants

Ahlgrim, David
Alduenda, Danilo
Alewine, Clifford
Alvardo, Juan
Ambriz, Julio
Ambrose, David
Andrews, Mitchell
Atkins, Nolan
Bailey, Austin
Bails, David
Baker, Nicholas
Ball, Zach
Barry, Cory
Becker, Andrew
Beckman, Michael
Bennett, Jace
Bernal, Joshua
Berry, Richard
Bihlmayer, Kris
Blaisdell, Harvey
Bloskas, Preston
Bonathan, Logan
Bonge, Dale
Bonge, Drew
Bramley, Cody
Breyer, Richard
Brown, Cody
Brown, Collin
Bryan, Danny
Bubeck, Sam
Budzinski, Andrew
Buri, Diane
Bursley, Matthew
Butler, Jared
Butler, Michael
Caithaml, Justin
Calander, Jacob

Campbell, John
Carrette, Jeremy
Choate, Christopher
Clark, Aaron
Clark, Brandon
Collie, Corey
Compton, Hayden
Conard, Tim
Coning, Alex
Coning, Duane
Coover, Kaylor
Courtade, Joseph
Cox, Bryce
Cox, Mike
Crain-Reutter, Jill
Creech, James
Crow, Jordan
Crow, Michael
Crowder, Chase
Cura, Jon
Currie, Jeremy
Cutts, Kevin
Danhauer, Kyle
Davidson, Joseph
Davis, James
Davis, Thomas
Delgado, Angel
Dickey, Nathan
Dolan, Marcus
Dreyer, Dillon
Dreyer, Jerry
Driscoll, Nicholas
Edson, Benjamin
Ellis, Andrew
Ellis, Jeffrey
Fair, Brin
Fleener, Trent

Gansten, Luke
Gonzales, Carlos
Gonzales, Gabriel
Grimm, Sammie
Guisinger, Robert
Hadley, Alexander
Hadwin, Robert
Hahn, Dale
Hambrick, Brian
Hankins, Tim
Harbin Iv, Charlie
Hardin, Ty
Hardison, Robert
Harmon, Clifford
Harrison, Cody
Harrison, Jeffrey
Harrison, Michael
Harrison, Nathan
Havens, Geoffrey
Henderson, Luke
Henningsen, Tyler
Higginbotham, Jb
Hill, John
Hill, Nathan
Hillenbrand, Joshua
Hodges, Trevor
Holtel, Brian
Hood, Joel
Hoover, Jordan
Hopper, Blake
Houser, Aaron
Hubbard, Rick
Huddleston, Ben
Huerter, Collin
Hutcheson, Greg
Irion, Maxim
Izatt, Michael

Jeslis, Matt
Johnson, Alexander
Johnson, Benjamin
Johnson, Blake
Johnson, Daniel
Johnson, James
Johnson, James
Johnson, Jared
Johnson, Samuel
Johnson, Seth
Jonas, Kyle
Jones, Jake
Joyce, Alan
Kaney, Matthew
Karsten, Jack
Keating, Michael
Keen, Kevin
Kennedy, Sean
Kerry, Devin
Kirmer, Richard
Kirschman, Jacob
Kirshman, Steve
Knox, Reece
Koudelka, Rob
Kresnicka, Matthew
Kresnicka, Thomas
Kretsch, Kyle
Lane, Jeremy
Langer, Cody
Leblanc, Cameron
Lee, Patrick
Lescallett, Brian
Lindgren, Eric
List, Torin
Lucerne, Jon
Lynn, Jacob
Malnar, Damien

Malnar, Gerry
Mangold, Tim
Matheney, William
Mccabe, Matt
Mccloud, Cody
Mccollon, Jesse
Mcdonald, Joseph
Mcginnes, John
Mcgonigal, David
Mcgrath, Linda
Mehl, Dave
Meng, Stephen
Merkling, Bradley
Merkling, Jeffrey
Midkiff, Luke
Miller, Tanner
Minshall, Aaron
Mitchelson, Will
Mitchem, Jackie
Modrall, William
Moore, Ben
Moore, Michael
Morrison, Stephen
Morse, Jerry
Morse, John
Mundy, Trent
Murphy, Michael
Nadeau, Sean
Naprstek, Dave
Naprstek, Jim
Neighbors, Bill
Nelson, Thomas
Nervig, Taylor
Newkirk, Timothy
Newkirk, William
Newlun, Christopher
Noel, Joshua

Odom, Johnny
Oldenburg, Jacob
Oldenburg, Roderick
Pape, Jonathan
Patrick, Tim
Penton, Conner
Perry, Ethan
Petty, Michael
Petty, Sam
Pike, William
Pilch, Justin
Powell, Bryan
Price, Eilanna
Price, Patrick
Radtke, Robert Jr
Raulin, Christopher
Rego, Jordan
Reisdorf, Jonathan
Reyes, Aaron
Rice, Forest
Robinson, Garrett
Rodriguez, Dimas
Roemisch, Mark
Romero, Ruben
Rook, Taylor
Routledge, Brett
Roy, Adam
Ryan, Sean
Rygiel, Jonathan
Ryniec, Duncan
Sakalis, Daniel
Salatino, Roland
Savitski, Marshall
Schatzel, John
Schmid, William
Scott, Will
Semple, Matthew

Sepper, Nick
Septant, Clay
Sevenich, James
Shillington, Logan
Sidesinger, Brett
Simmerman, Charles
Smith, Clayton
Smith, Garrett
Smith, Luke
Stanbary, Michael
Stanbary, Jr.,
    Michael
Stark, Steven
Stauffer, Max
Stenger, Stephan
Stevens, Robert
Tangen, Michael
Tates, Joshua
Tchon, Geoff
Teuscher, Tyler
Thornsen, Anthony
Tilley, Bill
Tucker, Jr., Stuart
Tully, Joshua-Paul
Tyler, Ryan
Tyler, Tim
Van Kerkhove, Mike
Veldhaus, Jacob
Veldhaus, Joshua
Vincent, Roger
Wagner, Matthew
Walter, Jonathan
Ward, Ethan
Warner, Andrew
Warner, Randy
Waters, Robert
Weckhorst, William

Weiss, Brian
Whicker, Tim
Whitehead, James
Whitehead, Zach
Wilcoxen, Dan
Williams, Cody
Withers, Caleb
Wood, Julian
Wuerdeman, Robert
Yancey, Michael

Manti-La Sal Staff

Abraham, Keith
Alger, Bruce
Armstrong, Joan
Arnold, J.J.
Arriola, James
Arvig, Andy
Ault, Glenn
Babb, Tim
Bailey, Bradley
Bajan, Greg
Barnes, Jeff
Barnett, Cody
Becker, Kyle
Berger, Marcus
Bichler, James
Bichler, Ronald
Bilyeu, Crystal
Bilyeu, Larry
Birch, Drew
Bissantz, Benjamin
Braddy, Ryan
Branigan, Jr., Michael
Breininger, Jeff
Bresnahan, Russell
Buchman, Joe
Bueltmann, Leilani
Byrne, Sean
Caipen, Lois
Carney, Alexander
Carney, Bruce
Carson, David
Chin, William
Christiansen, Gary
Chzanowski, Brian
Clark, Anthony
Clark, Anthony
Clasing, Mike

Clauson, Noel
Coleman, Sean
Cummings, Larry
Cummings, Sandra
Cunningham, Scott
Dickson, Jimmy
Dowty, David
Duncan, Jacob
Dworak, Joe
Dzialo, Russell
Edirisinghe, Chandana
Edwards, Jonathan
Fagan, John
Farbman, Eric
Ferris, Stephen
Fielder, Thomas
Fiori, Tony
Forrest, Michael
Frederick, Colton
Gabriel, Neil
Garay, Joel
Gaston, Grady
Gaston, Ryan
Graham, Stephen
Guinn, Thomas
Hambalek, Martin
Hampton, Steven
Harrell, David
Hawk, Ryan
Hedrick, Kenneth
Heimark, Steven
Hendricks, Mark
Hess, John
Hess, Letitia
Hipps, Joshua
Holland, Burl
Horne, Lynn

Hostmeyer, Mitch
Hughes, Clyde
Hunt, Joshua
Isaacson, Paul
Jensen, Paul
Johnson, Jo Ellen
Johnson, Ronnie
Jones, Aaron
Jones, Robert
Kaszuba, Karl
Keeler, IV, PJ
Knudsen, Jake
Kondziolka, John
Kropf, Mickie
Kurinsky, Jon
Landers, Dave
Larko, James
Leisz, Joe
Leisz, Robert
Lichota, Brad
Little, D. Scott
Little, Erik Scottt
Lombardo, Zach
Lopez, Juan
Martin, Thomas
Mason, Robert
McLeod, Scott
Mecham, Ryan
Mejia, Pattie
Memmott, BJ
Memmott, Kevin
Meuret, Andre
Meuret, Jean-Luc
Meuret, Timothy
Meyer, David
Miller, Dan
Miller, Dawn

Miller, Linda
Miller, Terrell
Miller, Trent
Murphy, Patrick
Norris, Mark
O Neill, John
Olsen, David
Olson, Lori
Otterstron, Tom
Overton, Danny
Overton, James
Palmantier, Chris
Palmantier, Jason
Palmantier, Marleny
Palmantier, Steven
Panko, Allice
Panko, David
Parker, Dale
Parker, Ed
Pepper, Brad
Pepper, Nicholas
Perkins, Mike
Peters, Michael
Petersen, David
Peterson, William
Pineo III, Charles
Powell, Steven
Price, Micheal
Pulley, Sam
Ramos, David
Reese, Ed
Renforth, Jack
Renforth, Jayson
Richardson, Jacob
Riedl, Tim
Romo, Raymond
Rose, Alexander

Rozek, Leonard
Rozek, Nicholas
Ruekberg, Jared
Ruekberg, Joe
Ryan, Brandan
Ryan, Larry
Saintisteven, Dane
Schaeffer, Brian
Schaub, David
Schrodt, Ben
Schultz, Logan
Schultze, Tracy
Severino, John
Sheren, Kirk
Silbiger, Steve
Smalley, Colin
Southwick, Jacob
Stanec, Skip
Stickel, Mark
Stilwill, Ben
Stoll, James
Stoll, Ryan
Sturges, Frank
Thomas, Dick
Thomas, Ian
Thomas, Jim
Topkis, Bill
Trick, Kaylene
Tschetter, Marty
Turk, Ryan
Ussery, Rickey
Van Wormer, Ray
Walsh, Bob
Walsten, David
Wedding, Daniel
Wellman, Jake
Wilder, Brian

Wilson, Leroy
Windsand, Jason
Winston, Malcolm
Winston, Moses
Winston, Martha

Manti-La Sal Participants

Anker, Nicholas
Arveson, Alex
Bacon, Caleb
Bankes, Derek
Barron, Christian
Barron, Ryan
Beals, Jason
Beard, Michael
Beard, Tyler
Benson, Daniel
Benson, Timothy
Bergh, Christopher
Bilyeu, Jacob
Bodenstab, William
Bosak, Stephen
Bostwick, Jeffrey
Bradford, Ryan
Brennam, Robert
Broadhead, John
Brost, Taylor
Brown, Allan
Bucchieri, Marc
Bucchieri, Vittorio
Buchans, William
Burnett, Arthur
Cagle, Zachary
Cambon, Jonathan
Carman, Daniel
Chaffey, Kellan
Chavez, Brandon
Cicero, Bobby
Clinton, Austin
Cloutier, Marcel
Conquest, Grant
Cooley, Jonathan
Curran, Joseph
Dennedy, Paul

Dobler, Paul
Dominguez, Jonathan
Eimen, Christy
Eimen, Donnie
Eimen, Tyler
Elliott, Matthew
Fassbender, Adam
Ferguson, Larry
Flug, Allen
Foley, Patrick
Fowler, Parker
Frederick, Andrew
Fredrick, Klynton
Furphy, Andrew
Gallo, Pam
Gamache, Jerod
Gibbs, Corry
Gibbs, Jennie
Goodale, Ray
Goodin, Rick
Grittman, Mason
Gross, Christopher
Guard, Jeffrey
Guymon, David
Hampton, Kyle
Hatvany, Thomas
Hazzard, Austin
Hedges, Ian
Hemp, Lucas
Hernandez, Oscar
Heston, Jonathan
Heston, William
Hickman, Kevin
Hissem, Timothy
Hoffman, Derek
Hoffman, Patrich
Holmes, Mark

Hosch, Damian
Irigollen, Ricardo
Isaals, Raymond
Jackson, Jeremy
Jenkins, Charles
Jenkins, John
Johnson, Eli
Johnson, Steven
Jones, Dalten
Jordan, Joshua
Kalny, Kenneth
Kalny, Kyle
Kilroy, Aaron
Kline, Zachary
Kous, Matthew
Kusmits, Jeffrey
Landers, Kevin
Leighhow, Christopher
Leighhow, Daniel
Leighhow, Robert
Linton, Dean
Locke, Cameron
Mandery, Alexander
Matson, Austin
McCormick, Michael
McGuckian, Shane
McLeod, Ian
McLeod, Rosana
McNeil, Kent
Means, Grant
Megaw, AJ
Meija, Sean
Midkiff, Luke
Morgan, Robert
Mortensen, Ryan
Mullins, Wesley
Murphy, Marshall

Myhre, Justin
Nance, Bryce
Neal, Aaron
Needham, Austin
Niemeyel, Ian
Olson, Zachary
Ostrich, Jeff
Ostrich, Richard
Palakiko, Micah
Palma, Daniel
Patrick, Shene
Pelland, Jon
Peterson, David
Pickering, Charles
Poncek, Jeremiah
Powell, Christopher
Purvis, Adam
Purvis, Timothy
Raffensperger, Kyle
Rakestraw, Johnathan
Rice, Farouk
Riehn, Robin
Seiter, Darin
Shannon, Jack
Shelhamer, Joshua
Shoemaker, Erin
Sitarski, Kyle
Spitzanagel, David
Spitzanagel, Ronald
Streib, Christopher
Tackett, Nick
Taylor, Dylan
Taylor, Jay
Thomas, James
Travis, Maui
Troup, Brenden
Troup, daniel

Vanhorn, Ryan
Wakeland, Kenneth
Walls-Barcellos, Austin
Wang, Derek
Weinrich, Steven
Whitinger, Ken
Wiesner, Timothy
Winston, Malsom
Winterton, Garth
Wynings, Dale
Zollinger, Mark

George Washington & Jefferson Staff

Absire, Justin
Addison, Merri
Albrecht, Blair
Aldrich, McLean M.
Alves, Robert
Anderson, Kevin
Anderson, Paul C.
Arnett, Walter
Baake, Jon H.
Bailey, Marcus
Barbieri, James R.
Beaupre, Paul
Becker, Andrew
Beebe, Sr., John A.
Bell, Ron
Benoit, Dustin
Bickford, Deanne
Bickford, Sebastian M.
Black, Alvan "Chip"
Bladen, Pete
Blake, Cyndy
Bledsoe, Michael
Bowdoin, Daniel
Briscoe, Jr., James
Brooking, Kevin W.
Brown, Timothy
Burden, Jimmie W.
Burke, Greg
Butler, Jack
Capp, Ray
Castillo, Gabrellia
Caves, Helen
Cebulski, Andrew F.
Chapman, Andy
Chilutti, Mark
Chow, Kay P.
Clements, Nelson

Coleman, David A.
Cotignola, Chris
Couce, John-Paul
Cowell, Michael
Davis, Bartley
Davis, Kenneth P.
Dearmin, Seth
DeMaria, Robert
Diaz, David
Diaz, Donald G.
Digirolamo, Nick
Donahue, Darrell W.
Draper, John
DuBois, Charles M.
DuBois, Dennis N.
Dukes, Nina
Dukes, Wayne
Durden, James P.
Dysart, Simeon
Easterling, Ryan
Eckle, Barry
Ellison, Don
Emery, Ralph
Eplee Jr., Robert "Gene"
Eure, Dwight
Falcon, Noel
Farmer, William J.
Fenty, Robert E.
Ferrier, Sean
Fielder, Graham
Fielder, Thomas
Finley, Jr., Edmund W.
Foote, John
Fore, Richard
Fry, Michael
Fullman, Doug
Garant, Ray

Gehring, Thomas
Gilmore , Justin
Goebeille, Fred A.
Gomez, T. Alex
Graves, Dustin C.
Gray, William
Greene, Cecile
Griffin, Ken
Groover, Michael
Hamlin, Craig KC.
Hamlin, Ronald D..
Harris, Andrew
Hicks, Nathan
Hobbs, Jon
Hodgkiss, Kara
Holinko, Alexander M.
Irving, Jeffrey
Ives, Perry N.
Jelsema, Ben
Johnson, Judy
Johnson, Skip
Johnson, Zachary
Jonasen, Jeffery Q.
Keener, Dennis C.
Keltner, John
Kline, Brian
Knaebel, Kenneth A.
Kupec, Michael A.
Landau, Geoff
Landau, Scott
Leet, Jr., William "Will"
Leet, Sr., William "Bill"
   A.
Lesser, Michael
Lesser, Quentin
Liakos, Thomas E.
Lombardo, J. Michael
   Chris.

Lynch, Michael W.
Marcus, Chris
Marks, M. Robert
Martello, Allen
Mauch, Anna
Maugeri, Joe R.
McCage, Robert E.
McCarthy, Justin D..
McColgan, James
McFarland, Roger
McGurk, Ellen D.
Mckenzie, Jonathan
McKinley III, Charlie E.
McKinney, J. Michael
McLeod, John E.
McLeod, Thomas H.
McNeely, Levi M.
McNeely, Michael J.
Mirisola, Mike
Mollit, Seth
Morrow, Jeffery A.
Morrow II, Jeffery A.
Nelson, Jamie
Niehoff, Zachary M.
Nowell, Craig
Nowell, Paul M.
O'Keefe, Michael
Olson, Bruce Allen Nilis
O'Neal, Christopher
Owen, Jr., Robert J.
Pankosky, Thomas W.
Papandrew, Devon A.
Papandrew, Gregory A.
Patterson, Elam M.
Pavlovich, Michael J.
Peavler, Nathan
Petty, James M.

Phillips, Harold
Pinna, Chaz
Pinna, Steve
Polk, Carroll
Porter, Chester H.
Quickenton, Phil
Rameriz, Anthony L.
Randolph, Rebecca
Randolph, Richard
Reddin, Thomas E.
Rephlo, John
Ribble, Frederick
Richards, Tom
Richards, Jr., Charles T.
Richter, Charles
Rivera, Orlando E.
Rivera, P.J.
Rogers, Gilbert
Rooney, Patrick
Rottenberg, Thomas H.
Ruh, Lawrence A.
Ryan, Joe
Sagoo, Rajpal
Sanders, Argus
Simpson, James H.
Singletary, Matthew T.
Singletary, W David.
Smith, Jr., Herb
Snipes, George
Soszynski, Daniel
Spath, James
Squicciarini, Phillip
St. Cyr, Jeff
Stahi, Levi
Standish, Raymond
Startzel, Pamela A.
Stephens, Jay L.

Stickle, Robert E.
Strebler, David
Sundergill, Jim
Sundergill, Linda
Surrett, David
Swedenburg, Keith
Swedenburg, Patsy
Sweeney, Brian
Sweeney, David J.
Targosky, Richie
Taricano, Tommy
Templeton, Tad
Thomas, John
Thompson, Chad
Thompson, Nicholas K.
Thompson, Sam
Thormahlen, Duane
Tillotson, Jason
Tobin, James J.
Tripp, Craig
Volk, Steve
Watson, Jr., Thomas E.
Weaver, Thomas
Weiner, Greg
Willis, Larry R.
Wilson, Matthew
Wiltenmuth, John
Wolz, Jason
Woodward, Jimmy
Wylie, Gary
Yates, Lorance (Randy)
Yates, Sandra K.
Zarrella, Vince (Zeke)
Zelenka, Mark
Zewalk, Mackie
Zung, Robert

George Washington & Jefferson Participants

Abraham, Kevin D.
Alford, Robert
Allen, Brian
Allen, Edward
Altrichter, Alex J
Alvin, Joe
Alvin, Jon
Alvin, Joseph
Ambrose, Joshua
Ance, Daniel C
Ankeny, Robert K
Ankuda, Zachary
Apastolico, Nicholas
Asta, Dominick
Aster, Jeffrey A
Athay, Billy Joe
Athay, Doctor Webb
Axton, Joshua
Axton, Nicholas M
Baber, Dorrian Me'Kal
Bain, James D.
Bain, James T.
Bancroft, James R.
Bancroft, William L.
Barton, Daniel
Bates-Smith, Joel
Batty, Alex
Bennett, John David
Berger, Jr., Marshall K.
Bib, Matthew D.
Black, Laramy
Black, Tyler G.
Blair, Nicholas
Blaser, John
Bontjes, Shayne
Borgman, Rex David
Brackin, Joseph Patrick

Brackin, William Joseph
Bragg, R. Jack
Brandel, III, Robert L.
Brandon, Marschal Austin
Brantley, Chris
Bray, James Alexander
Brewer, Matthew I.
Brueningsen, Eric
Brunold, Matthew
Brunson, Terryll Dean
Buford, Parker L.
Bullock, Victor R.
Buraczewski, Taylor James
Burnham, Josh
Burns, Grant C.
Burr, Evan
Burton III, Michael D
Calkins, David
Call, Gavin
Campbell, Ryan
Capp, Peter
Carson, Ryan
Carson, Steven D.
Castillonese, Peter T.
Celso, Sheldon
Chaban, Larry
Charters, William R
Chubb, Joseph Michael
Ciralli, Robert C.
Commendatore, Eric
Conner, Scott
Conver, Dallas
Cordle, Austin Blake
Cordle, Wendell Derek
Corpa, Jay A
Couch, William A

Craine, Andrew
Crawford, Richard Jordan
Crew, John
Criser, David E.
Cross, Douglas
Crowe, Robert E.
Crowe, Jr., Richard R.
Cunningham, Barry J.
Cunningham, Travis A.
Curtis, Corey
Cushing, Austin
Cutler, Jake
Dadiomoff, Roman J.M.
Daniels, Mark
Daniels, Matthew
Dannelly, Philip
Davis, Christopher
Davis, Christopher
Davis, Collin
Day, Hunter
DeHoff, Seth J.A.
Dehoff, Steven
Delgado, Angel M.
Denzier, Jon
DePaulis, Michael
Dolan, Jack T
Drake, Lawrence A.
Drake, Robert A.
Drake, Russell K.
Dufault, Andrew
Dunham, John
Echols, Peter
Ecklund, Todd
Edmondson, Graham
Edscorn, David
Ellis, Landon P

Eng, Arthur C.
Evans, Jack Craver
Evans, Olin Mark
Faison, Christopher W.
Felix, Julian J.
Feusse, James W
Filz, Michael
Finger, Wesley A
Fischer, Clay
Fite, Dylan T
Forcinito, Christopher
Fox, Carl J.
Franz, Byran
Franz, Nicholas
Fravel, Paul Logan
Freeman, Jubal
Fretwell, Joseph
Fritz-Lang, Andrew
Gallimore, III, Jerry S.
Gamble, John
Garcia, Patrick
Gaskin, Nicholas
Gawel, Brandon
Gaynor, Thomas D.
George, John Palmer
Gibson, Karl
Gibson, Travis
Gomez, Glenn G.
Gordon, Ethan Samuel
Gould, Jonathan C.
Green, Gabriel T.
Greene, Jr., Donald
Griffing, Timothy C.
Grinnan, Jr., James Allan
Gunnerson, Alex
Hagan, Allen W
Haig, Jonathan T.

Hammond, Robert Michael
Hand, Justin
Harris, Kyle
Haskett, Corey
Hawkins, Joseph
Hay, David M.
Hayden, Erik J.
Hayes, Richard
Haynie, Damon
Henley, Bernadine
Henley, David
Henry, James Andrew
Hicks, Cameron
Hicks, Zachary
Highsmith, Chaser R.
Highsmith, Russell A.
Hillis, Jonathan Daniel
Hoel, Joshua
Hogberg, Dennis H
Holley, Kevin B
Hotel, Edward
Hotel, Joseph M.
Hoy, Adam
Hoy, Andrew
Hoy, Paul A.
Hudgins, Thomas Derek
Hughes, Thomas Patrick
Huitt, II, Donald L.
Hume, James C.
Hunberger, Zachary
Hungerford, Jr., Celester L.
Hungler, John
Hunter, Vincent V.
Hunter, Vincent V.
Innes, James W.
Innes, Kevin M.

Isham, Matthew
Isham, Matthew
Izyk, Byron
Izyk, Byron
Jackson, Gregory
Jackson, Gregory
Jacquet, Bradly
Jaenicke, Matthew
Jaenicke, Thomas
James, Elliott
Jelincic, Mark
Jessup-Rebester , Nino Lavell
Johnson, Casey L.
Johnson, James
Johnson, Nathaniel S.
Johnson, Samuel
Johnson, William L.
Jones, Keith T
Jones, Michael
Joseph, Aaron C.
Joseph, Samuel A.
Joynes, Arthur
Jurkowski, Carl
Jurkowski, Michael
Kane, Sean Patrick
Kania, Robert C.
Kavanagh, Kyle
Kennedy, Kevin
Kerr, James
Kerr, Robert
Killebrew, Bradley
Kinnison, Benjamin
Kippenhan, Joseph
Koehler, Robert J
Kranock, Shane
Krushinski, Colin

Kudja, Colby D.
Kudja, Jose A.
Kuzmick, Kyle
LaGroth, Joseph Jared
Lampron, Joshua
Lang, Daniel
Larson, Nicholas
Lawson, Jacob
LeClaire, Daniel L
LeDuc, Daniel
Lee, Antwoine
Lee, III, Carlos M.
Leonard, Stuart Brice
Loflin, Mitchell
Longa, Alex
Longa, Gerald J
Lyle, Matthew S.
Malenfant, Charles
Malenfant, Jacob
Malora, Todd
Mandrapilias, Gus
Marino, Richard
Marshall, David P.
Marshall, Steven M.
Martenson, III, MD, Anders
Massari, Jr., Peter
Matroni, John O.
Maule, Jim
Maule, Robbie
McColgan, Jr., James J.
McCord, Adam
McDonald, Danny
McGlasson, Doug
McMullen, III, John R.
Melton, Ben
Mercer, Chrstopher

George Washington & Jefferson Participants

Mercer, Steven
Messerschmidt, Jonathan L
Midkiff, Luke
Miller, Nathaniel Tabor
Minello, Michael
Minnich, Charles
Misfeldt, Ron
Mohr, Jeremy L
Moore, Charles Andrew
Moppin, Jr., David
Moreno, Jr., Ramon J.
Moreno, Sr., Ramon J.
Morris, Mark H.
Morton, Neil R
Moskal, David
Murphy, Julian
Myers, Donald V.
Myers, Matthew J
Myers, Travis
Myler, Joseph
Naticchi, Christopher
Naticchi, James P.
Oldfield, Andrew Bryan
Omichinski, Paul C
Opthoff, John O.
Orlick, Jordan
Pacheco, Jose
Paeplow, Mark
Palmer, Jacqueline
Parent, Andrew M
Patalik, Joseph
Pate, David M.
Patenaude, Gabriel C.
Pavlovich, Michael J.

Peedin, Kenneth G
Peedin, III, K. G
Penzone, Constantine J.
Perry, Jr., Michael J.
Petruskevicius, Dylan
Pfeiffer, Richard A
Phillips, Jesse
Phinney, Sean
Pickens, Jr., Ronald D.
Pinna, Lydia
Piper, Zachary
Plumb, Adam A
Plunkett, Jr., Paul K
Pomy, Benjamin James
Pressler, Catherine L.
Pryor, Timothy W.
Puffenbarger, Christopher
Puffenbarger, Michael
Quinn, Edward A.
Rackliff, Jeannette
Rafferty, Chris
Ready, Diana K.
Reijmers, Peter
Reutiman, Robert James
Rex III, James C
Reynolds, Kevin
Reynolds, Sean N
Reynolds, III, Eric Jon
Richards, Daniel
Rigler, Edward
Risch, Kevin
Risnear, David P
Rivard, Michael

Rivera, Nomar E.
Rivera, Ramon L.
Roberson, Steven
Roberts, Scott
Rodriguez, Jonathan
Rodriguez, Skyler
Rogers, Jr., William Zimmer
Rooney, William Patrick
Ross, Thomas
Ruml, James A.T.
Rumley, Davis L
Russell, Mark A
Rutledge, Edward L
Ryan, Daniel Patrick
Scahill, Zachary
Schefelker, Andrew
Schirra, Trevor
Schnee, Brian L.
Schneeman, Michael D.
Schrager, Ira
Schrager, Leonard
Schuerle, Robert
Sell, Michael P
Semander, John
Shanks, William L.
Shannon, Zachary
Shearer, Robert
Shields, Steve
Shippee, Jr., Alan
Shrager, Ira
Shull, Tyler Clinton
Silliman, Jared
Slay, James S
Slocum, Jeremy

Sloop, IV, Robert F
Slowik, Nicholas J
Smedley, Devon
Smith, Johnny R
Snipes, Robert Shannon
Soles, Sr., Gregory C
Solomon, Michael
Spink, W. Craig
StaHari, Sean
Stamattades, Seth Tyler
Stambaugh, Parker
Stanford, Jason S
Starcher, Greg
Stehle, Jordon
Stephens, Greg
Stephenson, Benjamin Alexander
Stinton, Joseph
Strock, Daniel M.
Strock, Randall M.
Struble, Nicholas
Sukovich, Samuel
Talley, David
Tangfen, Craig
Terrio, Derek
Terrio, Kevin
Terrio, Rolf J.
Thomas, Matthew D.
Thompson, Nicholas
Toalson, Seth
Tomaine, Kris
Truly, Sean
Tucker, Steven W.
Turgeon, Christopher A.
Turnbulll, Ian

Turner, Michael D
Turner, William Patrick
Umberger, Brian
Underwood, Calvin T.M.
Vakil, Rohan
Valez, Marlon A.
Valle, Fernando
Valle, Wilson A.
Van Dyke, Jonathan A.
Vanche, Alex John
VanClief, Robert Douglas
Vannoy, Sean
Varela, Antonio
Veatch, Andrew
Verdell, Cydnei
Visokay, Adam
Voyles, Zackery G.
Wade, Kendall
Walters, Robert J
Warner, Chris
Warren, Ryan
Weaver, Michael S.
Welch, Sam
Wesley, Finger
Wetzel, Charlie
Wetzel, Christian
White, David
White, John T
Whitehill, Joseph
Whitman, Christian
Whittemore, Stafford Scott
Whittemore, Warren W.
Wiatt, Alex L.

Williamitis, Mathew
Williams, Benjamin
Williams, Clay
Williams, Ricky
Williams, Jr., James D.
Williamson, Kynndarrn S
Wilson, Shane D
Wingard, Andrew
Wirth, Mary
Wirth, Richard
Woerpel, Craig
Woerpel, Patty
Wood, Ezekiel
Wright, Jonathan
Writtenberry, Robert William
Yates, Charles
Yates, Corey
Yates, Lorance
Yates, Sandy
Yates, Scott
York, Courey
Yost, Jonathan

Shasta-Trinity Staff

Armstrong, Ross
Armstrong, Thomas
Armstrong, Vaughan
Atherton, Evan
Atherton, Tracy
Ault, Glenn
Baczkowski, John
Baker, Dominique
Barnwell, P. Craig
Benner Jr, Richard
Bishop, Vince
Black, Robert
Blankenship III, Otis
Bliss, Michael
Bohanske, Bob
Boileau, Patrick
Borysowski, Brian
Borysowski, Chester
Braden, Alex
Braden, Michael
Bradley, Sherri
Bradley, Steve
Brandenberger, Karl
Brock, Bradley
Brock, Robert
Brown, Paul
Bryner, Jeremy
Bushore, Ryan
Capps, Toby
Chaballa, Robert
Chandley, Garrett
Chandley, Scott
Chinn, Jack
Chun, Edwin

Cohen, Jonathan
Collett, Paul
Conner, Wil
Curtiss, Andrew
Curtiss, Corey
Danaj, Paul
Davidek, Steve
Davis, Bartley
Davis, Frank
Dawson, Kyle
DeCamp, Ken
Defeo, Donald
DeRemer, Ben
Desilet, Drew
Driscoll, Randall
Durbetaki, John
Durbetaki, Mark
Dydyk, Barry
Emery, Ralph
Epstein, Brad
Epstein, Jared
Farbman, Eric
Fischler, Kyle
Fosselius, George
Fulks, Calvin
Gaines, Steve
Galligan, Gary
Gana, Joshua
Garay, Joel
Gee, Edward
George, Michael
Giacalone, Samuel
Graham, Steven
Gray, Brian

Gray, Gary
Guilford, Jim
Harper, A. Frank
Harris, Brad
Hashiro, Brian
Hayashi, Ken
Higham, Dan
Hiszem, Paul
Hunker, Cheryl
Hunker, Dan
Ishizu, Mark
Jessop, Michael
Johnson, Steve
Keeler IV, Preston
Kern, Howard
Kirk, Dustin
Kitterlin, Patrick
Kiyohara, Kendall
Kiyohara, Mimy
Kolde, Kenneth
Kracht, Jason
Krawczyk, Linda
Kruse, Peter
Lacey III, Edward
Lacey IV, E. Davis
Landers, Paul
Lange, Paul
Lasko, Joey
Laudone, Matt
Lewis, Ivan
Loder, Del
Loweecey, James
Malaney, Tim
Marach, Noah

Marks, M. Robert
Mayfield, Bruce
McCullough, Cody
McKenna, Patrick
Meeds, James
Mellen, Jason
Meuret, Andre
Midkiff, Luke
Miller, Lenny
Miller, Leonard
Miller, Ned
Mitcham, Jarrell
Mo, Jo
Mo, Jonathan
Mosier, Kevin
Napoliello, Daniel
Niehoff, Zachary
Nix, Thomas
Noonan, Bruce
Ochsner, Nicholas
Pankosky, Daniel
Pares, Randy
Parks, Stephen
Pascucci, Dominic
Payne, Brian
Pierce, Brad
Piper, Jr, Hunter
Price, Thomas
Pulley, Samuel
Quick, Joseph
Radecki, David
Rapp, Renee
Reeder, Kyle
Reeder, Robert

Reeder, Shauna
Rendon, Jaime
Renfrew, Brian
Renfrew, Bruce
Renfrew, Elizabeth
Renfrew, Patrick
Renfrow, Kevin
Riley, James
Robert, Rene
Robinson, John
Roemer, Gail
Rogers, Andrew
Rogers, Angela
Rogers, Chris
Rubin, Jay
Ruekberg, Jared
Ruekberg, Joe
Ryan, Daniel
Schoenthal, Keith
Schwab, John
Shea, Joseph
Smith, Cookie
Snyder, Eric
Southwick, Jeff
Sowizdrzal, Judy
Sowizdrzal, Michael
Speer, Andrew
Staller, Mike
Stelting, Dale
Stoeckler, Robin
Striegl, Frank
Sutton, Ed
Taylor, Will
Taylor, Jr, Willbur "Bill"

Torn-Stabeno, Theresa
Trick, Kaylene
Vautrot, Lloyd
Wadford, Gene
Wadford, Judy
Walsh, Eli
Walters, Brady
Watson, Douglas
Wellman, Jake
Were, Theodore
Westmyer, Bob
Westmyer, Deanna
Westmyer, John
Wexler, Mike
Williams Jr, James
Winston, Jeffrey
Wolver, Chad
Wong, Robert
Woodard, Gregory
Wright, Tom
Yanni, William

Shasta-Trinity Participants

Abel-Jones, Christopher
Andrews, Lawrence
Andrews, Mitchell
Angstadt, Eric
Applegate, Brian
Armstrong, Mark
Arneson, Bob
Arnold, Ross
Austring, Richard
Auth, Sean
Averill, Daniel
Averill, Thomas
Baczkowski, William
Beck, Daryl
Bell, Michael
Bellomy, Samuel
Bergmann, Hans
Biggs, Gray
Biggs, Tyler
Blanc, Michael
Blocher, Andrew
Boileau, Elizabeth
Bona, Kevin
Bostian, Andy
Bowman, Shawn
Boyle, Zachary
Brodowsky, Taylor
Brown, Matthew
Brown, Michael
Brown, Stephen
Bryan, Thomas
Burgess, Zachary
Burkholder, Ernst
Butler, Thomas
Cabal, Timothy
Carcamo, Milton

Cardona, Gabriel
Carpenter, Greg
Carson-Small, Jeremiah
Carter, Michael
Carter, William
Castanzo, James
Champness, Seth
Clark, Kevin
Clark, Rick
ClichÈ, Dylan
Cluff, Lonnie
Cooley, Christopher
Coon, Christopher
Coronado, Willy
Cowley, Andrew
Cowley, AnnMarie
Culbertson, Justin
Dannenbaum, Willem
Davenport, Joseph
de Silveira, Caleb
Delao, Victor
DeRoche, Derek
Dinzeo, Mark
Dobbe, Sean
East, William
Eccleston, Jake
Einolf, David
Einolf, Davis
Fastnacht, Adolph
Figuers, Thomas
Fischer, Kevin
Fishburn, Callaghan
Fishburn, Guillermo
Fishburn, R. William
Fleenor, Joshua
Fletcher, Seth

Flint, Arthur
Follo, Mark
Forrest, Jeffrey
Frankland, Dylan
Freire, Raymond
Fry, Justin
Fullerton, John
Galchus, Matthew
Gallagher, Nicholas
Galligan, Gary
Garcia, Albert
Garcia, Jimmie
Garcia, Joseph
Gearing, Tyler
George, Parrish
Gibbons, Peter
Goss, Stuart
Grabner, Konrad
Graboyes, Kimberly
Grant, Raymond
Gray, Daniel
Grover Sr, John
Haas, Paul
Hackney, Jordan
Hagar, Alexander
Hager, J. Richard
Hansen, Eliot
Harkins, Zackary
Harrington, Patrick
Haskett, John
Haskett, Jon
Heberer IV, Raymond
Heberer III, Raymond
Hedrick, Dustin
Heller, Forrest
Heller, Loris
Henkenius, Nathan

Henshaw, David
Hibbs, Connor
Hickey, Jan
Hickey, Jason
Higdon, Thomas
Holman, Michael
Hontz, James
Hooks, Ryan
Horvath, Adrian
Iverson, Jake
Iverson, Jeffrey
Jackson, Gable
Jensen, Matthew
Johnsen, Paul
Johnson, Jake
Jones, Jake
Jordan, Kyle
Joyce, James
Kalista, Joshua
Kardos, Mark
Kartchner, Paul
Kartchner, Philip
Kasler, Bryan
Katris, Andrew
Kawamoto, Quinn
Kelly, Joseph
Kemp, Philip
Kemp, Richard
Kim, Michael
King, Steven
Kinney, Stephani
Kinzel, Dennis
Kirpes, Roger
Kline, Scott
Knudsen, Lucas
Kopczynski, Jason
Kupelian, Joshua

Kynerd, Alex
LaForge, Darrin
LaForge, Taylor
Largey, Sean
LaRue, Taylor
LeRoy, Ben
Littneker, Alan
Littneker, Randy
Loughridge, Tyler
Love, Jerry
Love, Parker
Ma, Patrick
Machschefes, Jacob
Major, Brian
Mapstead, Noah
Martin, Lucas
Martin, Thomas
Martine, Grady
Mason, Kyle
Mastel, Jacob
McAllister, Cole
McCreadie, Samuel
McGee, Brian
McInerney, Ian
McKinley III, Charlie
McLean, Michael
McNally, Morgan
McVey, Kendall
Mikita, Cody
Miller, David
Millerick, Michael
Mimnaugh, Bruce
Minor, Braden
Morgan, Taylor
Moscot, Joshua
Nelson, Eric
Nelson, Indy

Nelson, Jeffrey
Nelson, John
Ogle, John
Oravetz, Barthalomew
Palmiter, George
Palmiter, Sally
Partynski, Andrew
Patten, Chip
Patten, Wade
Peacock, Daniel
Peacock, William
Perry, Cole
Philichi, Dylan
Pina, Servando
Pingree, Geoffrey
Pitt, Jonathan
Popp, Christopher
Popp, Nicholas
Potter, Justin
Proffitt, John
Prokopt, Joshua
Proper Sr, Craig
Pusak, Kevin
Pusak, Warren
Ratuiste, Kevin
Ray, Geoffrey
Rayfield, William
Richter, Michael
Rider, Steven
Riekena, John
Rini, Christopher
Riordan, Justin
Robinett, Andrew
Robinson, Ryan
Ross, Thomas
Roth, Evan

Royer, Sylvain
Salinas, Mark
Sanchez, Jr, Daniel
Schoeller, John
Schroyer, Matthew
Schwab, John
Seiber, Barry
Sergojan, Jack
Sergojan, Karl
Sergojan, Volk
Shaffer, Nathaniel
Shaughnessy, Derrick
Shaw Jr, Clyde
Shea, Eric
Shoenech, Geoffrey
Short, Maxwell
Skandalis, Evan
Smith, James
Smith, Terry
Spidle, Edward
Stanford, Mitchell
Stauffer, Lucas
Strack, Fred
Strack II, Frederick
Stutts, Andrew
Stutts, Gary
Sullivan, Matthew
Sweet, Kyle
Talmage, William
Tarquinio, Robert
Taylor, Greg
Tes, Thony
Thorwart, Matthew
Timmerman, Eric
Truskdaski, Shane
Tseng, Brian

Tyger, Nicholas
Tyger, Russell
VanDyke, Robert
Vautrot, Jarod
Ward, Samuel
Waters, Sean
Weber, Jim
Weber, John
Widman, Matthew
Wissner, Brian
Woodward, Trevor
Worsham, Nathan
Worth, Andrew
Wright, Janet
Wright, Robert
Wright, T. Patterson
Wurfl, Ian
Yepez, Lucas
Yokono, Ryan
Young, Harry
Young, Nathan
Zeni, Joseph

Bridger-Teton Staff

Ahlberg, Jr., Richard (Rick)
Akin, Andrew (Andy)
Atkinson, Jr., Joe (Jeff) F.
August, Theodore (Ted)
Babb, Tim
Bailey, Marcus
Bajan, Greg
Beach, Gordon
Becker, Kyle
Beecher, Richard (Rick)
Beecher, Tim
Berger, Marcus
Bolles, Cortland
Bowen, Elizabeth
Bowen , Vince
Boyer, Keith
Braddy, Ryan M.
Bramlett, Terry
Brenner, Nathan
Bresnahan, Russell
Bridges, Lane C.
Brock, Bradley
Brooking, Kevin W.
Brooks, Charles C.
Brown, Dorothy (Dottie)
Bryant Jr., William R.
Bryant Sr., William R.
Bryner, Jeremy
Burinsky, Steve M.
Butler, Jack
Byrd, Jim
Byrne, Sean
Callahan, James "Jamie"
Cannon, Ryle M.
Carlson, David
Carpenter, Stephen C.

Carpenter, Jr., James R.
Carson, David
Cavalero, Michael A.
Caves, Helen M.
Cheesman, Ian
Cheesman, Kerry
Christopherson, Reid A.
Chrzanowski, Brian
Circus, Marc
Clasing, Michael D.
Coleman, Karlene
Colling, Spencer J.
Combs, Phillip
Cooper, Robert
Copeland, Charlie
Cox, Anthony
Crossland, Cashe
Crossland, Ian
Culver, Whit
Czech, Raymond R.
Daggett, Bill
Dahleen, David B.
Davis, Kenneth P.
Davis, Weldon (Cody) C.
Dawson, Logan C.
Dawson, Ryan E.
Deaton, Carl (Randy)
DeBusschere, Gerard
DePietro, Ronald J.
DeSoucy, M. David
Dickson, Jimmy
Dodson, Bruce
Dodson, Cody A.
Dowty, David C.
Dupaix, Michael R.
Dupaix, Steven C.
Dworak, Joe

Dziemian, Bob
Edwards, JD
Eliopoulos II, Thomas
Elliott, S. Tyler
Ellis, Bradley J.
Emery, Ralph
Enerson, Adam
England, Amos
Farrer, Clarke
Fife, Sam
Flynn, Robert J.
Friedrichsen, Aaron
Fromm, Adam
Fuhrman, Kurt
Galbraith, Jr, Robert B.
Gaston, Grady
Gaumond, Brett
Glenski, Joseph W.
Gole, Gary
Gregory, West
Griffin, Michael
Grogan, Michael
Grogan, Terry W.
Gross, Frederick
Grosz, Cortney
Grosz, Darnell (Deno)
Harris, Mark A.
Harris, William
Hatch, Nathan
Hayden, Ray
Heavey, James J.
Helland, Kevin
Hendricks, Mark
Hicks, Daniel
Hicks, Gary
Hipps, Joshua
Hobbs, Jon L.

Holland, Burl
Honan, Anmarie
Honan, Terry
Howe, Deborah L.
Howe, George M.
Hughes, Allen
Hunt, Joshua
Hutto, Skyler B.
Isaacson, Paul
Jackson, Daniel W.
Jackson, Will
Jendro, Kortney
Jenkins, Timothy L.
Jensen, Paul
Jilka, Brian
Johnson, Jo Ellen
Jones, Jeffrey C.
Kahler, Alexander
Kastner, Andrew
Keeler, Hannah S.
Ketel, Susan
Kinney, Jim
Kish, Adam R.
Kish, Robert (Bob)
Knudsen, Jake
Kraft, Warren P.
Kuhl, Zacheriah T.
Kuhlmann, Andrew
Kuhlmann, Kurt A.
Kunstman, Bobby
Lafitte, Bruce A.
Leavitt, Jonathan W.
Leet, William A.
Leet, William (Bill)
Leming, William H.
Lemley, Janssen W.
Lenker, Bill

Levitt, Bruce
Lewis, James S.
Lichota, Brad
Linderman, Andrew
Lombardo, Zach
Love, Loisann W.
Marks, M. Robert
Martin, Andrew P.
Mason, Robert
Mayer, Clyde
McCarty, Jeremy
McClurkin, Jared
McClurkin, Michael
McClurkin, Trevor
McCormick, William
McInnis, Thomas (Kyle)
McKinley III, Charles E.
McNeil, Kent
Meinke, Loren B.
Melin, Kurt
Meyer, C. Drew
Meyer, Charles D.
Midkiff, Luke
Miller, Carey L.
Miller, Daniel F.
Miller, Daniel
Miller, Jan
Miller, Terrel
Mills, III, Frank C.
Miske, Ryan
Moskal, David
Mullen, Stacy L.
Muller, Georg
Nachman, Ben
Nguyen, David
Nolan, Michael J.
Norris, Mark

Nuessmeier, Allen
Nygren, Bonnie
Nygren, Greg
Olson, Bruce A.
O'Neill, John (Jack)
Parker, Alan J.
Parker, Heather M.
Parmer, Michael D.
Peters, Gregg
Petz, Alan
Pomeroy, Brian
Porter, Andrew R.
Price, Michael
Pritchard, John
Richards, Bob
Richards, Donna
Richards, Randy W.
Richardson, Jacob
Riedl, Tim
Rodriguez, Robert W.
Rother, Albert J.
Rundman III, Sven J.
Sandrock, Chris
Schaeffer, Brian
Schaub, David
Schloss, Joe
Schmidt, John
Schmidt, Kenneth
Schock, Jerome J.
Schock, Jill C.
Schulte, Matthew A.
Seaborne, Doug
Seaborne, Sara
Seeton, Brian
Segersin, Carol
Segersin, Daniel T.
Segersin, Sean T.

Shapiro, Zachary
Sheren, Kirk
Siefker, Dale
Siefker, Mary Lou
Simmons, Jeff
Simmons, Mark
Skipper, Cory S.
Smith, Derek J .
Smith, Robert
Soltis, George M.
Southwick, Jacob
Speaks, Gregory
Spencer-Berger, Nick
St. Cyr, Jeffrey
Stevens, Jeffrey S.
Sturges, Frank
Suarez, Mario
Sundquist, David
Swedenburg, Keith
Swedenburg, Patsy
Syverson, Gib
Syverson, Karl
Syverson, Katherine
Tarbox, James
Taylor, Ben R.
Taylor, Darrell
Taylor, Timothy
Thomas, Ian
Thomas, Richard (Dick)
Thompson, Douglas A.
Thompson, Nathaniel L.
Tripi, III, Vince
Tschetter, Marty
Vanderwerker, Phil
Wangerin, Charles
Watson, Douglas
Wedding, Daniel

B-T Staff

Williams, Bruce
Wilson, Leroy A.
Winstead, Andrew
Winstead, J. Preston
Wogan, Keith
Yanni, William
Yoder, David
Zambon, J. Ryan
Zvonar, Marty

Bridger-Teton Participants

Adams, Doug
Adams, Priscilla M.
Adams, Scott F.
Adams, Steven
Ahrens, Brian
Ahrens, Michael
Ahrens, Stephen
Aikens, Eli
Aikens, Joshua
Albright, Mark
Allen, Alexander
Allinder, Thomas P.
Allison, Erik
Allred, Steven D.
Allred, Steven P.
Alward, Adam
Amerson, Robert D.
Ammons, Sam
Andrea, Kellen
Andrews, Lawrence
Andrews, Mitchell
Anstett, Robert
Aravich, Evan W.
Aravich, William P.
Arndt, James B.
Arnold, Christopher M.
Atherton, Tracy
August, Aaron
Ayer, Austin
Ayvar, Khalil
Azzaro, Michael
Azzaro, Steven
Banegas, Quinton
Banegas, Travis W.
Barcellos, Mark
Barker, Gail
Batchelor, Daniel
Batchelor, Joshua

Batchelor, Rod
Battaglia, Charles
Battaglia, Michael
Baughan, Ross
Baum, Phillip
Baumgartner, Eric
Bazonis, Mike
Beard, Colin
Beard, Martin
Beatty, Jacob
Beatty, Mark
Beaudry, Mark
Beaudry, Phillip
Becker, Logan
Beetz, Mark
Beggs, Alex
Behrens, Isaac
Bendel, Derek James
Bendel, Jr., Donald James
Benito, Jose
Benito, Joseluis
Bennett, Joseph
Bennett, Joshua
Bennett, Mason
Bernaiche, Don
Bernaiche, Kyle
Bernhard, Judith Lynn
Beutel, John W.
Beyer, William
Binversie, Nathaniel Randall
Bishop, Kilton
Bitker, Landon
Bitker, Taylor T.
Blackstad, Marcus
Bleam, Pascal
Bleam, William
Bohon, Charles Spencer

Boire, Jr., Michawl Matthew
Boldt, Lori
Boldt, II, Joseph E.
Boles, Tanner E.
Bolyard, Craig
Boomer, Adam Lee
Borchers, Bruce
Bouyea, Nicholas
Bowlus, Bruce
Bowlus, John
Boydstun, Samuel D.
Braddock, John J.
Brault, Cody
Breaux, Patrick W.
Bredesen, Tyler
Brickel II., Steven John
Briggs, William
Broeker, Andrew
Brosler, Jason
Brown, Allan
Brown, John B.
Brown, Montana
Brown, Trevor James
Brown, William C.
Brunell, Nicholas F.
Bruner, David Thomas
Brunold, Matthew J.
Bruvelis, Stefan
Brywig, Austin Carl
Brywig, Dale M
Buechel, Jeffrey P.
Buell, David A.
Bundgaard, Avery
Buono, Mathew J.
Burbank, Michael
Burch, William C.
Burke, Timothy M.
Burrell, Keith

Buso, Neil
Butcher, Patrick D.
Byland, Matthew
Byland, Orrin
Cadena, Alexander
Cadena, Edward
Campbell, Cameron F.
Card, Michael
Carley, Benson I.
Carley, Jr., Dale H.
Carlson, Benjamin
Carlson, III, Charles
Caron, Luc
Cary, Ian M.
Cary, John C.
Case, James
Cass, David Wayne
Cass Jr, David Wayne
Cavahaugh, Joe
Cavender, William F.
Chandler, Matt
Chapdelaine, Louis
Chapman, Beverly L.
Chapman, Linda
Chapman, Raymond
Chilton, John
Chilton, Robert
Chisholm, Elijah
Ciralli, Robert A.
Ciralli, Robert C.
Clark, Deborah M.
Clark, Taylor
Claussen, Michael
Claussen, Tom
Cleghorn, Ian M.
Cole, William P.
Comell, Chris
Comell, Joshua

Compton, Brian
Conkey, Michael J.
Cook, Garrett
Cook, Morgan S.
Cook, Stephen
Copeland, Brad
Corey, Kyle D.
Cotton, Jr., Thomas Michael
Cowden, Steven
Cozad, Logan
Cramer, Daniel
Crantek, Dalton L.
Cristobal, Abubakr
Crocco, Jake
Crutchfield, Christopher
Crutchfield, Steven
Cumming, Andrew R.
Cyrus, June H.
Dahl, Chris
Dahlgren, Kristian
Dahlgren, Todd
Day, Patrick R.
DeMare, Nathan
Demeules, Alexander
Dennis, Dalton
Dennis, Walter E.
Derbes, Michael
Deuyter, Michael
DeVault, Douglas
Dickerson, Jake
DiIulio, Dylan R.
DiIulio, Robert J.
Dilks, Christian
Dilks, Ethan
Dilks, Justin
Dismukes, Brian
Dismukes, Wilson
Dixon, Eric

Dooley, Nathan
Dougall, Michael J.
Doughty, Patrick
Drewilz III., Antony W.
Driscoll, Don A.
Driscoll, Philip
Dryden, Hunter
Dulaney, Bryan
Dunlap, Neill
Dysart, Simeon
Edwards, James B.
Ehrlich, David
Eisenschenk, Jack
Elfring, Michael B. G.
Elwell, Adam
Elwell, Jr., Joseph O.
Enser, Daniel
Etchberger, Henry
Fallon, Eric Michael
Farrand, Mark
Farrar, Jack C.
Farrell, Bruce
Faucette, Tyler
Ferguson III., Charles E.
Figlar, Charles A.
Finlay, Jerrrod S.
Fisher, Landon
Fitzgerald, Mark
Flatt, Brian H.
Flatt, Joel
Flowers, Kurt Harvey
Fordham, Jonathan W.
Forster, Matthew
Foster, II., Richard
Frederick, Caleb
Frederick, William S.
Freemon, Bob
Freemon, Susan

Bridger-Teton Participants

Frees, Drew
French, Bryce
French, Thomas
Friedel, Matthew J.
Furbee, Eric
Furniss, Evan
Gaddis, Steven
Galchus, Matthew K.
Gardner, Preston
Garofano, Joseph
Generous, Alex
Gibbens, Cody
Gillette, Howard Michael
Gilliland, Micah K. B.
Gleason, Connor
Gleiser, Jeffrey J.
Gleiser, Scott A.
Glotfelty, William Thomas
Glotfetty, Timothy A.
Glover III., Roger H.
Goehrig, William B.
Goepfert, William F.
Golden, Jack
Gomez, Chris
Gordon, Ryan C.
Gorsline, Bradley
Gorsline, Jim
Grabowski, Connor
Gray, Matthew
Gray, Spencer
Green, Jr., Calvin
Greene, Logan
Greer, James
Grim, Allen
Grismer, Dane Ashton
Grismer, Timothy Paul
Groce, Tyler J.
Gross, Clark

Gross, Eisen C.
Gross, Garrett
Grothe, Mark A.
Guilmette, Alexander P.
Guilmette, Paul A.
Gutowski, Nicholas
Haile, Ethan H.
Hall, Andrew J.
Hall, Clay
Hall, Kirk W.
Hall, Peggy
Hamilton, Gordon L.
Hamilton, Loren Paul
Hargett, John
Hargett, Michael
Harker, Cody
Harold, Colton
Harris, Neil
Hartford, Zakary D.
Harvey, Logan J.
Hatch, Christopher
Haugdahl, Trevor
Hayes, Patrick M.
Haymore, Jr., Jonathan D.
Heid, Vincent
Heins, Jonathon
Heishman, Gary J.
Henderson, Philip L.
Hendricks, Addison
Henning, Mark
Herrington, Michael M.
Higham, David
Hill, Brandon A.
Hills, Ryan C.
Hines, Derek Jon
Hinson, Spencer Henry
Hintz, Tyler S.
Hirschmann, Robert D.

Hjermstad, Andrew
Hoff, Paul
Hogenkamp, Jimmy
Hogenkamp, Markus
Holder, Christopher
Hone, Joshua
Hornick, Fred
Horwitz, Philip
Hubbard, H. Lee
Huber, Christopher
Hudlow, David
Hughes, Robin
Huguley, Harold G.
Hurlburt, Eric
Hurley, Bryan E.
Hurley, Daniel J.
Hutto, Brad
Hyla, Gary D.
Hynes, Michael Carlton
Ingram, Wayne
Ives, Graham
Jackson, Jeffrey R.
Jacobs, Matthew M.
Jacobs, Michael J.
Jagielski, Alex
Jagielski, Carolyn
Janochoski, Joseph
Jennes, Coleman
Jensen, John H.
Jesberger, Adam
Jesberger, David
Johnson, Douglaus
Johnson, Steven
Johnston, Shawn Lee
Jones, Lawrence
Jones, Sean
Jones, Zachary
Kaiser, Kevin

Kalla, Daryl
Kane, John
Kantor, Kody
Kastner, Barbara
Keim, Mitchell
Keiser, Andrew
Keiser, Dale
Kelling, Nicholas
Kelly, Brendan
Kendl, Drew
Kendrick Jr., John
Kennerly, Rob
Kent, Christopher A.
Kent, David
Kent, Matthew
Kerzman, James
Kiihr, Brian T.
Kiihr, Thomas
King, Matthew Richard
Kline, John H.
Kline, Seth P.
Klock, Andrew
Klutts, Daniel
Knak, Kevin
Knott, Alfred
Knott, Andrew
Knowlton, John B.
Knudsen, Charles R.
Koenig, Andrew
Kominsky, John
Korabek, Kyle
Kotowski, Christopher
Kowalewski, Alan
Kox, Andrew
Kramer, Timothy
Krasula, Andrew
Krasula, Jim
Kraus, Michael

Kraus, Ryan
Krygier, Stephan Zygmunt
Kuehn, Paul
Kuehn, Steven
Kuhn, Zachary Matthew
Landrum, Chad M.
Landrum, Derek
Landry, Gregory
Lapierre, Justin T.
Lapierre, Ronald A.
Laursen, Charles T.
Laursen, William G.
LeClaire, David E.
LeClaire, Irene A.
Lesinski, Francis David
Lewiston, Eric
Lewiston, Joel
L'Heureux, Brian T.
Lieby, Matthew
Lillemo, Kenneth W.
Lillich, David
Lillich, Mason
Linner, Tyler
Lloyd, Adam
Lloyd, Ramona
Loeb, Andrew
Logan, Trent
Lohr, Matthew
Lokken, Peter
Long, John M.
Long, Lenny
Losee, Julie
Losee, Mark
Losee, Matthew
Loutsch, Brandon
Lovallo, James Patrick
Lowe, William C.
Luff, Christopher

Lukowski, Spencer
Lumpkins, Jeffrey
Lumpkins, Robert E.
Lundquist, Edward H.
Lundquist, Thomas I.
Lynn, Anthony
Lyon, Brandon
Lyons, Douglas S.
Lyons, Porter X.
Macchiaroli, Peter
Macchiaroli, Jr., Carmine
MacDonald, Ian
Macpherson, Tracy
Maddox, Samuel
Magill, Jacob
Mahuna, Josh
Maitwe, Patrick
Malarbi, Nicholas T.
Maley, Jr., Daniel P.
Malley , Jonathan
Malley, Jr, James
Mancl, Andrew
Marcotte, Tyson J.
Markley, Scott
Martinson, Kurt L.
Masin, Dustin Charles
Mayer, Bruce
Mayer, Jonathan
McAninch, Cheston
McCarran, Keil J.
McClain, Patrick
McCloskey, Andrew C.
McCloskey, Christopher J.
McCloskey, Timothy C.
McCool, Jim
McCranie, Willie D.
McCrossan, T. Daniel
McCurry, Luke e.

McEniry, Sean
McFall, Jonathon
McFall, Matthew
McGough, Mark T.
McLean, Patrick A.
McMahon, Morgan
McMillan, William
Meadows Jr., Brian
Melin, Nicholas
Merijanian, Aaron
Messman, Karil Michel
Meyer, Robert W.
Meyers, Derrick S.
Michalek, Carlin James
Michel, Matthew
Mierzejewski, Christopher
Milani, Stephen
Miles, Brendan
Miller, Daniel
Miller, David
Miller, Gary S.
Miller, Jason A.
Miller, Jaymes H.
Miller, Joseph H.
Miller, Matthew Ryan
Miller, Morgan
Miller, Robert G.
Miller, Ryan R.
Milligan, John
Milligan, Larry
Milliigan, Dave
Mims, Owen R.
Mitchell, Alex P.
Mohlman, Kenneth
Molek, Joe
Molesworth, Drew
Molina, Jeffrey L.
Molina, Stephen R.

Bridger-Teton Participants

Moore, Benjamin Robert
Moore, Matthew
Morabito, Connor
Morel, Michael
Morgan, James
Morgan Jr., Jon C.
Morgo, Zachary T.
Morlang, Jr., Robert E.
Morris, Tim
Morris, William R.
Morton, Ronald D.
Mott, Daniel James
Moulton, Alexander
Muir, Patrick J.
Mullen, Blaine L.
Mullen, Donovan
Mulligan, Ryan
Muncy, Jeffrey L.
Munn, William Thomas
Murphy, Julian
Murphy, Thomas A.
Newby, Paul
Niebaum, John J.
Nielson, Michael
Nolan, Thomas J.
Nolf, Ryan
Nonhof, Karen
Noonan, Francis
Nowag, Joseph W.
Nunn, James C.
Nunn, R. James
O'Connell, John Kevin
Oliver, Alexander
Oliver, Benjamin
Oliver, Christopher
Oliver, Mark
O'Neill, David
O'Neill, James
Ostwald, Patrick

Owens, Edwin B.
Pacchiana, Oliver
Pahalek, Chris
Parker, Benjamin
Parker, Pablo N.
Parks, Damien
Parks, James H.
Parnell, Rudolph Arnold
Parrott, Eric
Patenaude, Grant C.
Patterson, Sammie A.
Paulson, Bruce
Peck, Richard A.
Peck, Travis
Pedersen, Nicholas M.
Perkoski, Barbara A.
Petersen, Austin Riley
Petersen, Marie
Peterson, Jack L.
Pfeiffer, Jonathon
Pfeiffer, William
Phettepace, Christopher
Phillips, Keegan
Phillips, Lon
Pibal, Thomas L.
Piccone, Christopher
Pierre, Steve
Pikul, Kevin
Pillsbury, Connor M.
Pillsbury, Kelly
Piper, Andrew
Plew, Brian
Poaletti, Daniel
Poaletti, Kevin
Pollinger, Jake R.
Poole, Geoffrey
Poppe, Nathanael W. A.
Powell, Christopher S.
Powell, Frank R.

Prado, Jeffrey
Prado, Jon
Prado, Juan
Prather, Alex
Price, Jr., Arthur A.
Pryer, Timothy W.
Pulk, Tyler
Quigley, Brian
Quinn, Coleman
Quinn, Patrick H.
Quisenberry, Cindy
Quisenberry, Henry
Quisenberry, Jonathan
Radzicki, Christopher
Ramberger, Nathan
Randall, Orray J.
Raslich, Eric
Rassler, Eli N.
Reardon, Zachary T.
Reijmers, Peter
Reilly, Bryan
Rekemeyer, John
Rhines, Timothy
Rhines, Tristan
Rhines, Tyler
Rice, Farouk
Riedesel, Shawn
Riviere, Michael C.
Riviere, Michael R.
Robb, Daniel
Robb, Michael
Roberts, Christian
Roberts, Edward
Robinson, Gary
Rochette, Gary
Rodgers, Carl L.
Roen, James P.
Roepke, Jason
Roncone, Vincent

Ross, Scott J.
Rueger, Andrew J.
Rueger, Bruce F.
Rundman IV., Sven J
Runkel, Travis
Ruth, III., H. L.
Saralecos, Jarred
Saufferer, Ryan
Saxon, Joseph C.
Saxon, Phyllis D.
Schadrack, III, William C.
Schmidt, Michael
Schnabel, Isaac
Schodorf, Brandon
Schroeder, Luke
Schulze, Erik
Schulze, John
Schulze, Kurt
Schweitzer, Nicholas
Segler, Bryce
Selim, Maha
Senoffsky, Douglas
Sexton, Matthew C.
Sheets, Corey
Sherman, Mark
Shermetaro, Janice
Showalter, Curtis
Showalter, Matthew
Sibley, Gabriel
Sibley, Jeff
Simmons, Robert G.
Simmons, Will S.
Skoff, Robert
Slattery, David S.
Slay, George P.
Slay, James J.
Smalley, Logan
Smith, Benjamin H.
Smith, Michael

Smith, Spencer
Smith, Taylor W.
Solazzo, Ronald M.
Solazzo, Jr., Stephen P.
Solt, Benjamin David
Soszynski, Michael
Staab III, William J.
Staab Jr., William J.
Stading, James R.
Stallings, Curtis
Stanton, John M.
Stauffer, Raymond
Steele, John
Steffens, Jonathan
Steinberger, Michael
Steinberger, Thomas
Stewart, Michael E.
Stoppa, Thomas M.
Stottlemyer, Kyle
Stugelmayer, Cody L.
Sullivan, III., Jerry
Sutterfield, Thomas
Swafford, Matthew
Swartz, Tom
Swedberg, Carl
Swisher, Douglas
Syfrett, Daniel
Syfrett, David Lee
Tamas, David
Tang, LaVerne
Tang, William T.
Tanner, Seth Walter
Taylor, Aaron P.
Taylor, Chris
Taylor, David
Temple, Thomas
Teuscher, Ryan
Teuscher, Tyler
Thompson, Ferron W.

Thompson, Jesse W.
Thompson, Travis
Thorne, Don
Thorne, Tyler
Tochterman, Michael R.
Tomberlin, Jack A.
Tracy, Joshua
Tracy, Jr., John M.
Tripi, Jonathan
Tripi, II., Vince
Tunheim, Michael Jay
Turbeville, Ryan
Turner, Douglas E.
Turner, Harrison
Tuttle, Christian
Vail, Tracen E.
Valentine, Benjamin
Valentine, John
Valle, Wilson A.
Van Haren, Ben
Van Helten, Michael
Van Ness, Lowell T.
Van Steenbergen, Barry
Van Steenbergen, Dylan
Vasko, Benjamin
Vine, Brandon
Vinson, Devin
Vinson, Lane D.
Votava, Russ
Wallace, Matthew
Walls-Barcelos, Austin
Warring, Christopher
Warszynski, Jacob J.
Warszynski, Jeffrey A.
Wasmer, Benjamin
Wasserman, Kevin
Watkins, Christopher
Watkins, David
Watson, Justin B.

Weaver, Christopher
Webb, John T.
Webb, Timothy
Webster, Matthew
Wester, Zachary A.
Whiteard, Sharon
Whiting, Marc
Whitney, Jason
Whittier, Cody
Wieting, Ernie
Wildes, Benjamin W.
Williams, Kelly H.
Willis, Steven C.
Wills, Michael
Wilson, Jeramey
Wilson, Jessey
Wilson, Michael G.
Wohler, Austin
Wolf, Alexander James
Wolf, Justin
Woods, Adam Wayne
Woods, Sidney Wayne
Wright, Daniel
Wright, Gary W.
Wright, Wesley
Wysocki, Neil A.
Yarbrough, Brian C.
Youngkin, Michael
Yuan, Fernando
Ziegler, Zachary
Zillig, Christopher
Zimmerman, Eric
Zomcik, Stephen
Zukic, Jacqueline
Zukic, Travis James
Zwetskoot, Henry
Zylla, Aaron P.
Zylla, Leonard R.
Zylla, Nathan

Instructor Corps

David C Dowty
Instructor Corps Director

Burl E. Holland
Assistant Director of Operations

Paul Jensen
Assistant Director of Training

David Schaub
Assistant Director of Administration

Tim Babb
Greg Bajan
Kyle Becker
Marcus Berger
Ryan Braddy
Russell Bresnahan
Sean Byrne
David Carson
Brian Chrzanowski
Mike Clasing
Jimmy Dickson

David Dowty
Joe Dworak
JD Edwards
Grady Gaston
Mark Hendricks
Joshua Hipps
Burl Holland
Joshua Hunt
Paul Isaacson
Paul Jensen
Jake Knudsen

Brad Lichota
Zach Lombardo
Robert Mason
Dan Miller
Mark Norris
John ONeill
Michael Price
Kent McNeil
Jacob Richardson
Tim Riedl
Brian Schaeffer

David Schaub
Kirk Sheren
Colin Smalley
Jacob Southwick
Frank Sturges
Ian Thomas
Marty Tschetter
Daniel Wedding

Photo Contest Winners

Mark Twain

Recreation

1st Place Youth - Tim Hankins, Waupecan Lodge

2nd Place Youth - Josh Veldhaus, Ku-Ni-eh Lodge

3rd Place Youth - Josh Kirlin, Kiskakon Lodge

1st Place Adult - Judy Johnson, Mikanakawa Lodge

Campsite

1st Place Youth - Mitch Andrews, Wapashuwi Lodge

2nd Place Youth - Tim Hankins, Waupecan Lodge

3rd Place Youth - Josh Kirlin, Kiskakon Lodge

1st Place Adult - Judy Johnson, Mikanakawa Lodge

2nd Place Adult - Ryan Meador, Tamegonit Lodge

Scenic

1st Place Youth - Sean Tighe, Echeconnee Lodge

2nd Place Youth - Josh Kirlin, Kiskakon Lodge

3rd Place Youth - Tim Hankins, Waupecan Lodge

1st Place Adult - Ryan Meador, Tamegonit Lodge

2nd Place Adult - Judy Johnson, Mikanakawa Lodge

Work

1st Place Youth - Josh Veldhaus, Ku-Ni-eh Lodge

2nd Place Youth - Tim Hankins, Waupecan Lodge

3rd Place Youth - Josh Kirlin, Kiskakon Lodge

1st Place Adult - Ryan Meador, Tamegonit Lodge

2nd Place Adult - Judy Johnson, Mikanakawa Lodge

Manti-La Sal

Recreation

1st Place Youth - John Kondzi, Wipala Wiki Lodge

2nd Place Youth - Erik Little, Elkuta Lodge

1st Place Adult - Dawn Miller, Tu-Coobin-Noonie Lodge

2nd Place Adult - Charles Pineo, Egwa Tawa Dee

3rd Place Adult - Russ Dzialo, Sikhs Mox Lamonti Lodge

Campsite

1st Place Youth - John Kondzi, Wipala Wiki Lodge

2nd Place Youth - Ron Bichler, Tom Kita Chara Lodge

3rd Place Youth - Erik Little, Elkuta Lodge

1st Place Adult - Bill Topkis, Elkuta Lodge

2nd Place Adult - Charles Pineo, Egwa Tawa Dee

3rd Place Adult - Dawn Miller, Tu-Coobin-Noonie Lodge

Scenic

1st Place Youth - Ron Bichler, Tom Kita Chara Lodge

2nd Place Youth - Tim Hissem, Tiwahe Lodge

1st Place Adult - Robert Lynn Horne, MD, Nebagamon Lodge

2nd Place Adult - Bill Topkis, Elkuta Lodge

3rd Place Adult - Charles Pineo, Egwa Tawa Dee

Work

1st Place Youth - Erik Little, Elkuta Lodge

2nd Place Youth - Tim Hissem, Tiwahe Lodge

3rd Place Youth - Steven Heimark, Nebagamon Lodge

1st Place Adult - Dawn Miller, Tu-Coobin-Noonie Lodge

2nd Place Adult - Christy Eimen, Cahuilla Lodge

3rd Place Adult - Charles Pineo, Egwa Tawa Dee

George Washingon/Jefferson

Recreation

1st Place Youth - Robert Shearer, Nentego Lodge

2nd Place Youth - John Robert Gamble, Eswau Huppeday Lodge

3rd Place Youth - Robert Kania, Amangamek Wipit Lodge

Campsite

1st Place Youth - Roman Dadiomoff, Amangamek Wipit Lodge

2nd Place Youth - Robert Shearer, Nentego Lodge

3rd Place Youth - John Robert Gamble, Eswau Huppeday Lodge

1st Place Adult - Keith T. Jones, BobWhite Lodge

Scenic

1st Place Youth - Robert Shearer, Nentego Lodge

2nd Place Youth - John Robert Gamble, Eswau Huppeday Lodge

1st Place Adult - Keith T. Jones, BobWhite Lodge

2nd Place Adult - Nicholas Thompson, Ktemaque 15 Lodge

Work

1st Place Youth - Robert Shearer, Nentego Lodge

2nd Place Youth - John Robert Gamble, Eswau Huppeday Lodge

3rd Place Youth - Roman Dadiomoff, Amangamek Wipit Lodge

1st Place Adult - Keith T. Jones, BobWhite Lodge

2nd Place Adult - Edward Hotel, Blue Heron Lodge

Shasta-Trinity

Recreation

1st Place Youth - Chris Rogers, Wauna La Mon'tay Lodge

Campsite

1st Place Youth - Mitch Andrews, Wapashuwi Lodge

2nd Place Youth - Chris Rogers, Wauna La Mon'tay Lodge

1st Place Adult - Lawrence Andrews, Wapashuwi Lodge

Scenic

1st Place Youth - Bryan Kasler, Wauna La Mon'tay Lodge

2nd Place Youth - Mitch Andrews, Wapashuwi Lodge

3rd Place Youth - Chris Rogers, Wauna La Mon'tay Lodge

1st Place Adult - Angela Rogers, Wauna La Mon'tay Lodge

Work

1st Place Youth - Bryan Kasler, Wauna La Mon'tay Lodge

2nd Place Youth - Mitch Andrews, Wapashuwi Lodge

3rd Place Youth - Chris Rogers, Wauna La Mon'tay Lodge

1st Place Adult - Lawrence Andrews, Wapashuwi Lodge

Bridger-Teton

Recreation

1st Place Youth - Scott Markley, Hunnikick Lodge

2nd Place Youth - Andrew Koenig, Colonneh Lodge

3rd Place Youth - Alex Allen, Chickagami Lodge

1st Place Adult - Stephen Carpenter, Mikanakawa Lodge

2nd Place Adult - Ken Lillemo, Totanhan Nakaha Lodge

Campsite

1st Place Youth - Scott Markley, Hunnikick Lodge

2nd Place Youth - Jerrod Finlay, Coosa Lodge

3rd Place Youth - Andrew Koenig, Colonneh Lodge

1st Place Adult - Jim O'Neill, Nacha Nimat Lodge

2nd Place Adult - Brian Dismukes, Ahoalan Nachpikin Lodge

3rd Place Adult - Tom Murphy, Octoraro Lodge

Scenic

1st Place Youth - Scott Markley, Hunnikick Lodge

2nd Place Youth - Jerrod Finlay, Coosa Lodge

3rd Place Youth - Brian Yarbrough, Yah-Tah-Hey-Si-Kess Lodge

1st Place Adult - Blaine Mullen, Tahosa Lodge

2nd Place Adult - Brian Dismukes, Ahoalan Nachpikin Lodge

3rd Place Adult - Ken Lillemo, Totanhan Nakaha Lodge

Work

1st Place Youth - Scott Markley, Hunnikick Lodge

2nd Place Youth - Alex Allen, Chickagami Lodge

1st Place Adult - Tom Murphy, Octoraro Lodge

2nd Place Adult - Brian Pomeroy, Susquehannock Lodge

3rd Place Adult - Brian Dismukes, Ahoalan Nachpikin Lodge

ArrowCorps⁵ Donors

Toby Capps
J. Robert Coleman, Jr.
David F. Jenkins
E. Hadley Stuart, Jr.

Conduit Corporation
Dominion Resources
Enterprise Rent-A-Car
ExpressJet Corporation
FleetWeather
John Deere
MeadWestvaco
National Fish & Wildlife Foundation Pulling Together Initiative
National Forest Foundation Matching Awards Program
Rocky Mountain Power
Snap On Incorporated
Shell Oil Company
Vienna Lawnmower
Zee Medical, Inc.

Partners

Mark Twain
Camp Wisdom, Circle Ten Council
Chesapeake Valley Water
Dan Busee & Mark Wilbur
John Deere Tractors
KBR Construction Services
Kelly & Company First Responders
Lowe's Home Improvement
MedSafe Safety & Medical Supplies
Missouri National Guard
Pendragon Design & Art Work
St. Johns Airflight Medical Service
St. Johns Hospital, Emergency Dept
Sysco Foods
Texas National Guard
U.S. Forest Service-Mark Twain-MINGO Workers
U.S. Forest Service-Mark Twain Headquarters
U.S. Forest Service-Mark Twain-Ava District
U.S. Forest Service-Mark Twain-Cassville District
Vienna Lawn Mower

Manti-La Sal
Bureau of Land Management
Carbon County Weed Department
Castleland Rural Conservation & Development Council
City of Huntington
DOW Agrosciences LLC
Emery County School District
Emery County Sheriff's Office
Emery County Water Conservancy District
Emery County Weed Department
National Park Service
Skyline Cooperative Weed Management Area
UAP

U.S. Forest Service Ferron Price Ranger District
Utah Deparment of Agriculture
Utah Department of Foresty Fire & State Lands
Utah Department of Natural Resources
Utah Division of Wildlife Resources
Utah Partners for Conservation and Development
Utah State Institutional Trust Lands
Utah State University Extension Service

George Washington & Jefferson
Alleghany County
Alleghany Highland Chamber of Commerce
Arritt Funeral Home
Augusta Hotshots
City of Covington
Covington Lumberjacks
Douthat State Park Employees
Flatwoods Job Corps Center
Garelick Farms of Maine
HP Hood LLC
James River District, GW/J National Forest
Mountain Electronics
Roanoke Valley Greenways
Town of Clinton Forge
Town of Iron Gate
VA Backcountry Horsemen of America
Valley Area Shared Trail Network
Virginia Dept of Conservation & Recreation

Shasta-Trinity
Backcountry Horsemen of California Shasta-Trinity
Shasta College
Shasta County Board of Supervisors
Shasta-Trinity National Forest personnel

Bridger-Teton
Dean Foods
Friends of the Pathway
Jackson Chamber of Commerce
Jackson Hole High School
Lost Creek Ranch
Meridian Group
Pathfinders for Greenways
Reading Bus Lines
S&J Renovations
Snow King Resort
Teton Conservation District
Teton County School District #1
Teton County Weed and Pest
Teton Stage Lines
Teton Trail Riders
Thrifty Car Rentals
Town of Jackson
Transportation Group LLC
Wells Fargo Bank
Wyoming Army National Guard
Wyoming Game and Fish

U.S. Forest Service Personnel

U.S. Department of Agriculture Personnel
Rey, Mark

U.S. Forest Service National Personnel
Beaty, Tim
Finlayson, Karen
Gage, Steve
Holtrop, Joel
Kimbell, Abigail
Madden, Eugene
Manning, Gloria
McGee, Deidra
Schwartz, Jamie
Steinke, Dave

Mark Twain U.S. Forest Service Personnel
Adams, Halle
Adams, Justin
Bond, Tim
Boness, Todd
Bray, Reggie
Chad, Keith
Cox, Kevin
Dry, Chance
Farenbaugh, Jenny
Haberl, Ken
Halpern, James
Hardman, Beth
Harris, Ande
Hoogendoom, Derick
Horner, Robert
Kocher, Josh
Maijala, Shawn
May, Steve
Mendenhall, Sandy

Miles, Kathy
Mosher, David
Murrell, James
Nettie, Sittingup
Oliver, Doug
Olsen, KC
Olson, Marg
Page, Roberta
Paxton, Bill
Register, Jess
Rein, Darla
Reynolds, Jeremy
Soard, Jerry
Stewart, Moke
Strong, Paul
Swirin, Ty
Thacker, Tasha

Mark Twain U.S. Forest Service Mingo Workers
Bryant, Patrick
Elledge, Joseph
Karr, Antonio
Metcalfe, Mavick
O'Brien, Todd
Phillips, Greg
Price, Jimmy
Sneen, Marcus
Sumler, Aaron
Sumler, Chris
Lang, Keith
Waldner, Robert

Manti-La Sal U.S. Forest Service & Other Agency Personnel
Brown, Pamela
Healy, John
Nyman, Meisa
Ivory, Karl
Bureau of Land Management
Worthington, David
National Park Service

George Washington & Jefferson U.S. Forest Service Personnel
Bodkin, Mike
Coulson, Dawn
Emerson, Brian
Higgins, Liz
Hyzer, Maureen
Jackson, Gerry
Lipps, Woody
Merritt, Rebecca
Mohney, Sharon
Norman, Yvonne
Rose, Chris
Sheridan, Pat
Smestad, Steve
Thomas, Lorraine
Tripp, Mike

Shasta-Trinity U.S. Forest Service Personnel
Heibel, John
Heyward, Sharon
Jordan, Kathleen
Kellogg, Ken
Naser, Steve

Bridger-Teton U.S. Forest Service Personnel
Bacon, Stephanie
Balboni, Mike
Cernicek, Mary
Clark, Greg
Dustin, Rick
Dykehouse, Rod
Fogel, Dave
Franklin, Barb
Hamilton, Niffy
Hatch, Jeff
Haydon, Steve
Hegg, Sara
Hershey, Terry
Kallusky, Eli
Larson, Karol
Lindeberg, Teri
Merigliano, Linda
Ozenbeger, Jim
Peck, Chris
Porter, Rich
Shaw, Jess
Shields, Bill
Truitt, Trish
Upton, Cliff
Williams, Leslie
Zardus, Heidi